John
Steinbeck

The People to Know Series

Madeleine Albright
First Woman
Secretary of State
0-7660-1143-7

Neil Armstrong
The First Man
on the Moon
0-89490-828-6

Isaac Asimov
Master of
Science Fiction
0-7660-1031-7

Robert Ballard
Oceanographer Who
Discovered the Titanic
0-7660-1147-X

Willa Cather
Writer of the Prairie
0-89490-980-0

Bill Clinton
United States
President
0-89490-437-X

Hillary Rodham Clinton
Activist First Lady
0-89490-583-X

Bill Cosby
Actor and Comedian
0-89490-548-1

Walt Disney
Creator of
Mickey Mouse
0-89490-694-1

Bob Dole
Legendary Senator
0-89490-825-1

Marian Wright Edelman
Fighting for
Children's Rights
0-89490-623-2

Bill Gates
Billionaire
Computer Genius
0-89490-824-3

Jane Goodall
Protector of Chimpanzees
0-89490-827-8

Al Gore
Leader for the
New Millennium
0-7660-1232-8

Tipper Gore
Activist, Author,
Photographer
0-7660-1142-9

Ernest Hemingway
Writer and Adventurer
0-89490-979-7

Ron Howard
Child Star &
Hollywood Director
0-89490-981-9

John F. Kennedy
President of the
New Frontier
0-89490-693-3

Stephen King
King of Thrillers
and Horror
0-7660-1233-6

John Lennon
The Beatles and Beyond
0-89490-702-6

Maya Lin
Architect and Artist
0-89490-499-X

Jack London
A Writer's
Adventurous Life
0-7660-1144-5

Barbara McClintock
Nobel Prize
Geneticist
0-89490-983-5

Rosie O'Donnell
Talk Show Host
and Comedian
0-7660-1148-8

Christopher Reeve
Hollywood's Man
of Courage
0-7660-1149-6

Ann Richards
Politician, Feminist,
Survivor
0-89490-497-3

Sally Ride
First American Woman
in Space
0-89490-829-4

Will Rogers
Cowboy Philosopher
0-89490-695-X

Franklin D. Roosevelt
The Four-Term
President
0-89490-696-8

Steven Spielberg
Hollywood Filmmaker
0-89490-697-6

John Steinbeck
America's Author
0-7660-1150-X

Martha Stewart
Successful
Businesswoman
0-89490-984-3

Amy Tan
Author of
The Joy Luck Club
0-89490-699-2

Alice Walker
Author of
The Color Purple
0-89490-620-8

Simon Wiesenthal
Tracking Down
Nazi Criminals
0-89490-830-8

Frank Lloyd Wright
Visionary Architect
0-7660-1032-5

John Steinbeck

America's Author

Donnë Florence

Enslow Publishers, Inc.

40 Industrial Road	PO Box 38
Box 398	Aldershot
Berkeley Heights, NJ 07922	Hants GU12 6BP
USA	UK

http://www.enslow.com

Library of Congress Cataloging-in-Publication Data

Florence, Donnë.
    John Steinbeck : America's author / Donnë Florence.
        p. cm. — (People to know)
    Includes bibliographical references (p.   ) and index.
    Summary: A biography of the California writer, discussing his childhood,
hardships, friendships, travels, works, and awards, including the Pulitzer and
Nobel Prizes.
    ISBN 0-7660-1150-X
    1. Steinbeck, John, 1902–1968—Juvenile literature. 2. Novelists, American—
20th century—Biography—Juvenile literature. [1. Steinbeck, John, 1902–1968.
2. Authors, American. 3. Nobel Prizes—Biography.] I. Title. II. Series.
PS3537.T3234Z638   1999
813'.52—dc21
[B]   98-36412
                                                                    CIP
                                                                     AC

Printed in the United States of America

10 9 8 7 6 5 4 3 2 1

To Our Readers:
All Internet addresses in this book were active and appropriate when we went to press.
Any comments or suggestions can be sent by e-mail to Comments@enslow.com or to
the address on the back cover.

Illustration Credits:
Center for Steinbeck Studies, San Jose State University, pp. 18, 32, 68, 71,
79, 105; Library of Congress, pp. 49, 54, 56, 63; Mr. Pat Hathaway,
California Views Historical Photo Collection, pp. 9, 21, 38, 40, 76; National
Steinbeck Center courtesy Pat Hathaway Collection, p. 6; National Steinbeck
Center courtesy Valley Guild-Steinbeck House, Salinas, California, p. 14;
courtesy National Steinbeck Center, Salinas, pp. 44, 88, 90, 100; National
Steinbeck Center, Salinas, © Stuart Schwartz, p. 110; *New York Then and
Now: 83 Manhattan Sites Photographed in the Past and Present* (New York:
Dover Publications, Inc., 1976), p. 26; *The Depression Years As Photographed
by Arthur Rothstein* (New York: Dover Publications, Inc., 1978), p. 60.

Cover Illustration: Underwood Photo Archives, S.F.

Contents

John Steinbeck

The Best-Laid Schemes o' Mice an' Men

All John Steinbeck wanted in the winter of 1936 was peace and quiet. He had always known he would not like being famous, and now he knew he was right. His first successful book, *Tortilla Flat*, was published the year before. Ever since, people he did not know had been writing him letters and telephoning. Some of them walked right up and knocked on the front door of his little house in Pacific Grove, California. The interruptions distracted him from working on the new story he wanted to write.

What he had in mind, he wrote to a friend in February, might be a children's story. "I want to recreate a child's world," he wrote, "not of fairies and giants but of colors more clear than they are to adults, of tastes more sharp and of the queer heart-breaking feelings that overwhelm children in a moment."[1] Children's stories did not have to be happy, Steinbeck thought. Children are not happy all the time, he reminded his friend.

The story Steinbeck wanted to tell was not a happy one. It was about homeless men who traveled from one California ranch to another in search of work. There were hundreds of these men in the early 1920s in the Salinas Valley. The men helped with planting or harvesting crops at one place. When the work was done, they moved on to help at another ranch a few miles away. They usually walked or hitchhiked, carrying their bedrolls and a few possessions in a bundle—or "bindle"—on their backs. They were often looked down on by the ranchers' families and others. Some people called them bums or "bindle stiffs."

Steinbeck had known men like these. During high school and college vacations, he had worked alongside them on ranches near his home. Now he wanted to tell their story in *Of Mice and Men*. He would tell the story of George Milton and his friend Lennie Small, two bindle stiffs who dream they will have a farm of their own one day. Lennie has the body of a big, strong man but the mind of a young child. He accidentally kills small animals because he does not know any better than to pet them too hard. Lennie's size, strength, and slow thinking keep getting him and George into trouble. It is not Lennie's fault, George knows, but their best-laid schemes of owning a farm will always be a dream that will not come true.

As the story took shape in Steinbeck's mind, it

In Of Mice and Men, *Steinbeck created a story about the homeless men who traveled from farm to farm looking for work. The farmers in the Salinas Valley depended on these migrant workers to plant and harvest crops like the field of lettuce above.*

turned out not to be a good one for very young readers. Steinbeck thought *Of Mice and Men* would be a good story for working men. They understood the hard life of men like George and Lennie. Working men did not read novels, Steinbeck knew. They did sometimes attend plays in the towns near where they worked. Steinbeck decided to tell the story mostly through dialogue, so that it could also be acted out on a stage. By March 1936, he had the story figured out and was ready to begin writing, but the interruptions kept getting worse.

Steinbeck and his wife, Carol, decided they would have to move. They bought some land in Los Gatos, about fifty miles away. Carol designed a new house for them. At the beginning of May, Carol Steinbeck went to Los Gatos to supervise the building of the house. Now Steinbeck was alone most of the time in Pacific Grove. He did have a young puppy, a setter named Toby, with him. Toby was as much company as Steinbeck wanted. Work on *Of Mice and Men* was going quickly.[2]

Late in May Steinbeck came home one evening to find that Toby, alone in the house, had "made confetti" of the manuscript. "There was no other draft," Steinbeck wrote to his agent.

> *I was pretty mad but the poor little fellow may have been acting critically. I didn't want to ruin a good dog for a manuscript I'm not sure is good at all. He only got an ordinary spanking.*[3]

Steinbeck began rewriting. Building continued at the Los Gatos house. By July the house was finished enough for the Steinbecks to move in. They named their new home "Steinbeckia." The only heat came from a fireplace in the living room and a small stove in Steinbeck's workroom. The new house did not have running water or electricity yet, but Steinbeck thought he would like roughing it for a while.

He did not like roughing it for very long. The workmen finishing the house made noise that distracted Steinbeck during the day. Writing at night by the light of a kerosene lantern was hard on his eyes. He got up early in order to have as many daylight hours as he could for writing. Writing kept him too busy to chop long logs into shorter pieces for the fireplace. Steinbeck would bring whole logs into the house and push them farther into the fireplace as the end burned.[4]

By September, the book and the house were finished. The workmen had gone, but peace and quiet had not come to Steinbeckia. Fans had already begun finding their way to the new house. They broke the lock on the gate. One woman barged in and asked Steinbeck to get her daughter into the movies. "Dance for the man, Mildred," she said.[5]

Steinbeck had laid his pads and pencils aside when he finished *Of Mice and Men*. Now he took up his woodworking tools. He carved a new gate he hoped would keep uninvited visitors away. "Arroyo del Ajo," it said. "Steinbeckia" was no more. The new name for the house was Spanish for Garlic Gulch.

Of Mice and Men was published in 1937. It became a best-seller and is still one of Steinbeck's best-loved works. Steinbeck wrote a separate stage version, which won the New York Drama Critics' Circle Award for Best Play of 1937. The first movie version was released in 1939, and the story was filmed again in 1981 and 1992.

Like all of Steinbeck's best works, *Of Mice and Men* grew out of people and places he had known. The land, the sea, the plants, animals, and ordinary people of California were wonders of nature to Steinbeck from his earliest days.

California Boy

John Steinbeck was born February 27, 1902, in the front bedroom of his parents' home in Salinas, California. Young John was named after his father, John Ernst Steinbeck, a flour mill owner and manager who would later become the treasurer of Monterey County. The Steinbecks were not rich, but the family was never broke or poor. Steinbeck's father did business with local farmers and grew flowers and vegetables in his own garden. He taught John to know the many kinds of plants and animals that thrived in Monterey County.

Steinbeck's mother, Olive Hamilton, had been a teacher at a tiny red schoolhouse south of Monterey before she married John Ernst Steinbeck. Like other

John Steinbeck was born in this large Victorian house in Salinas, California.

women of that time, she left her job when she married, and focused on being a wife and mother. For Olive Steinbeck, this meant making sure that her children were always properly dressed, well behaved, and good students. She wanted them to be models of middle-class respectability.

Both of John's parents were fond of literature. Before John could read by himself, they often read aloud to him. They read from the Holy Bible and from popular literary works such as *Alice in Wonderland*, *Pilgrim's Progress*, and *Treasure Island*. The tale that would become John's lifelong favorite was Sir Thomas Malory's *Morte d'Arthur*, the story of King Arthur and the Knights of the Round Table.

John Steinbeck had two older sisters. Esther was nine when John was born. Elizabeth, who was always known as Beth, was seven. Esther and Beth were excited to have a baby brother. They pampered John and fussed over him. Like their parents, Esther and Beth also read to young John. John would grow up closest to his younger sister, Mary, who was born in 1905. He was closer in age to Mary, so she became his regular playmate when they were children. He remembered Mary this way many years later:

> She rode like a cockleburr, was the best pitcher anywhere near her age on the West side of town, and was such a good marble player that the season had to be called off because she had won every marble in town.[1]

John learned to read at home, before he started school. Even before he could read, John enjoyed looking at the words and pictures in books. When he was four, John discovered that *high* rhymed with *fly*. His fascination with language was born.[2]

The Steinbecks' handsome Victorian house stood near the center of Salinas, the seat of government for Monterey County. The county stretched from the fertile Salinas Valley to such famous oceanside places as Monterey, Carmel, and Big Sur. The towns, farms, seashore, and mountains of Monterey County would one day become the settings for some of John Steinbeck's best-loved stories.

Salinas was "a town of wooden frame houses, the trading center of the valley, the social center of the whole world as we knew it," Steinbeck remembered later. There was "always something to do," he said, in the town of about twenty-five hundred people.[3]

Few families in Salinas owned cars in those days. People from outlying farms rode horses or drove horse-drawn buggies to town. Cars fascinated John from his first view. He wrote:

> *The first car I remember . . . was, I think, a Reo. . . . It was owned by a veterinary who got himself a bad name in Salinas for owning it. He seemed disloyal to horses.*[4]

Neither John nor his father could be accused of disloyalty to horses. Despite his interest in cars, what young John wanted was a pony of his own. When John was ten, his father presented him with Jill, a red pony who became John's pride and joy. When John and Mary acted out their own versions of the daring Knights of the Round Table, Jill was their noble steed. With helmets and shields made of cardboard, John and Mary dueled with strips of wood. They spoke a secret language they had partly invented and partly borrowed from *Morte d'Arthur.*[5]

John used the pony, and the privilege of riding her, to cement his friendships with other Salinas children. One of these was a boy named Glenn Graves, who had lent John a saddle. Graves later remembered John as a sort of ringleader among their friends. John would think up adventures for himself, Glenn, Mary, and the other children.

For a while, these adventures involved a man known as one of Salinas's misers. The story around town was that this man kept a hidden stash of gold and money. The children believed it. They peeked into his windows at night, hoping to catch sight of him counting his money. Sometimes they made spooky noises for the thrill of seeing the man jump up and make dramatic speeches to an audience that was not there.[6]

Besides the house in Salinas, Steinbeck's parents owned a cottage in Pacific Grove, a little town near the tip of the Monterey Peninsula. The cottage, about twenty-five miles from the house in Salinas, was used mainly for family getaways. John's Grandmother Hamilton had a home a few blocks away. Grandmother Hamilton believed in fairies and leprechauns. Thanks to the stories she told, John believed in them too, just as he believed in the magic of King Arthur's Merlin and the miracles of the Bible.

Traveling between Salinas and Pacific Grove in the family's horse-drawn surrey, John Steinbeck learned the landscape of Monterey County. The Salinas Valley

Here we are. Mary, John + Jill — Salinas Aug 28.0

John and his younger sister, Mary, enjoyed acting out stories about King Arthur and his knights. Jill, the pony, was their noble steed.

was a patchwork of farms and fields connected by unpaved country roads. The low mountains between the valley and the ocean were home to a wilder kind of nature. Cypress trees twisted by fierce winds grew amid rock outcroppings where mountain lions sometimes prowled. On the other side of the mountains lay Monterey Bay and the seaside towns of Pacific Grove and Monterey.

Pacific Grove was a small residential community, but Monterey had been the first capital of California. Its Ocean View Avenue was lined with shops, churches, office buildings, and warehouses. Near the docks were large canneries where local fishermen brought their catch of sardines. This stretch of Ocean View

Avenue was known to Monterey residents as "Cannery Row." Monterey was a sophisticated, built-up place compared with Salinas. The people were different, too. Monterey was filled with people who made their living from the sea—fishermen, sailors, and cannery workers.

Both the cottage in Pacific Grove and the house in Salinas offered quiet places to read as Steinbeck was growing up. His favorite book remained *Morte d'Arthur*. Malory's story of King Arthur and his noble Knights was written in an old form of English that fascinated young John. He marveled over old-fashioned spellings of familiar words and words that were no longer used. The language was an adventure, just as the story was. After the Bible, the story of King Arthur provided some of the most important ideas for Steinbeck's later works. He would use its themes of group strength, honor, and brotherhood in two of his early novels, *Tortilla Flat* and *In Dubious Battle*. He dreamed of writing his own version of King Arthur's story.

By the time he entered high school, John had decided on a career as a writer. His parents encouraged his writing, but they did not imagine then that he would make a career out of it. His father would bring home used ledger books from the office. John liked to write his stories on any blank pages that were left. The ledgers had stiff cardboard covers that made it easy to write in them wherever he went. He could carry a ledger and a pen or pencil to a quiet place under a tree and did not need a table or desk to write on.

Tall and thin, with fair hair and blue eyes, the teenaged John Steinbeck had a prominent nose and large ears. He considered himself *too* thin, his nose and ears *too* large to be attractive. Like many people, he was shy in some ways. He hated public speaking, and making new friends seemed harder than it should be. John did make friends, but he sometimes felt he was forcing himself to do it. He joined the staff of *Gabilan*, his high school newspaper, and was on the school's swimming and basketball teams. These activities introduced him to other students who shared his interests in writing and sports.

During summers and high school breaks, John worked, mostly on nearby farms. He ran cultivators, bucked grain sacks, and did other kinds of odd jobs around cattle or in sugar refineries. The jobs allowed John to earn his own money. They satisfied the strong work ethic his parents had instilled in all their children. They gave him the chance to observe and learn about people and lifestyles that were different from his own.[7]

John Steinbeck graduated from Salinas High School in 1919. That fall he began attending Stanford University in Palo Alto, about eighty miles from Salinas. He enrolled in classes that interested him—mainly English and marine science—rather than the prescribed set of courses he needed to earn a bachelor's degree.[8] Steinbeck was eager to get on with his writing career. He did not want to spend time studying things he did not feel he needed to know. From time to time, he lost interest in college and dropped out for a while.

Pure idleness was out of the question for anyone in the Steinbeck family. During breaks from college

Fishermen brought their daily catch to the canning factories near the Monterey docks. The canneries faced Ocean View Avenue, and locals called the street "Cannery Row."

Steinbeck worked. Short stretches of hard, physical work were nearly always available on California ranches, especially at harvest time.

John Steinbeck could return to college or to his parents' home when a harvest ended, but while he worked on the ranches, he lived among migrant farmhands. He would one day turn this experience into a famous short novel and play, *Of Mice and Men.*

Steinbeck was never a regular student at Stanford, but he was not an outsider, either. He made friends with college roommates and classmates such as Carlton ("Dook") Sheffield, Amasa ("Ted") Miller, and Webster ("Toby") Street. These friends and others welcomed him back each time he returned to college.

Whenever he could, Steinbeck enrolled in Stanford courses that would help him write better. One of these was a class in short-story writing taught by a professor named Edith Mirrielees. This was the kind of education Steinbeck was looking for at Stanford. Mirrielees saw real talent in Steinbeck. She read and critiqued his work, always ending on an encouraging note. The encouragement made her criticism easier to take, and Steinbeck usually followed her advice. Steinbeck and Mirrielees remained friends for many years after he had left Stanford. He recalled her always as his best Stanford teacher.[9]

In class or out, Steinbeck created stories. Two of these, "Fingers of Cloud" and "Adventures in Arcademy," appeared in the *Stanford Spectator*, the student newspaper. Others remained in Steinbeck's notebooks and in his head. Some of them would emerge later as parts of his books.

By 1925, most of Steinbeck's Stanford friends had graduated. Steinbeck had not graduated, but he decided it was time for him to leave college, too, and begin making his mark as a writer. Edith Mirrielees advised him to go to Europe, where he could live cheaply while he devoted time to his writing.[10] Many aspiring young writers of the 1920s—including Ernest Hemingway and F. Scott Fitzgerald—had been given similar advice from others. They had taken the advice, but John Steinbeck had his own ideas.

3

Years of Struggle

John Steinbeck sailed for New York City in November 1925. New York was the literary capital of the United States and obviously the right place for a writer. He paid for his ticket by working on board the ship, helping to prepare and serve meals to the officers and crew. When the ship stopped in Panama, Steinbeck went ashore. This was a chance to absorb the look and feel of the place for a book he was planning to write about a famous pirate, Sir Henry Morgan.

In New York City, Steinbeck rented a small, cheap room. He planned to write when he was not working to earn money for rent and food. He got a job wheeling barrows of bricks and concrete to the workers who were building the new Madison Square Garden at Eighth Avenue and Fifty-third Street. The construction site was cold and dark, and the work was hard and dangerous. Steinbeck quit after just a few weeks.

Steinbeck's uncle Joe Hamilton came to town then. Uncle Joe was an advertising executive in Chicago. He and Steinbeck agreed that a job as a reporter might be good training for an aspiring writer. Hamilton had connections in the publishing business and got Steinbeck a job on *The New York American.* Steinbeck was not a good reporter, he admitted.[1] He was more interested in literature than journalism.

Steinbeck showed some of his short stories to a man named Guy Holt, who worked for a publishing house, Robert McBride and Company. The McBride company was interested in publishing work by unknown but talented new writers. Holt encouraged Steinbeck to write more stories, enough for a book, and then come back. Fighting tiredness, Steinbeck labored in his few hours outside work to produce a story collection for Robert McBride and Company.

By the time Steinbeck returned with his completed stories, Guy Holt had left Robert McBride and Company. Steinbeck spoke to a new editor, who rejected the book with barely a glance at it. Steinbeck just could not earn and save enough money to quit working and devote himself full-time to writing. After a year, he gave up the plan of becoming a New York City writer. "The city had beaten the pants off me," he confessed later.

In 1925, John Steinbeck went to New York City with dreams of becoming a writer.

Whatever it required to get ahead, I didn't have. I didn't leave the city in disgust—I left it with the respect plain unadulterated fear gives. And I went back to my little town, worked in the woods, wrote novels and stories and plays. . . .[2]

With the help of his Stanford friend Toby Street, Steinbeck found what seemed to be an ideal job back in California. In the fall of 1926 he became the caretaker of an estate near Lake Tahoe. He looked after the mountain lodge of a wealthy family named Brigham while the owners lived in San Francisco for most of the year. This job required short spurts of hard physical work, including chopping wood for the stove, which was the only source of heat in his cabin.

Other than keeping himself warm and fed, the job was mostly house-sitting, making sure intruders stayed away. Steinbeck had plenty of quiet time alone. He could read the books the Brighams kept in a fine library in the main house, and he could work on his own writing. Steinbeck was diligent and businesslike about his writing. If writing was going to be his life's work, he had to treat it like a job. He made sure that he wrote every day, and he kept track of how many words he had written.

By now Steinbeck was moving ahead with the Henry Morgan novel. It had begun as a short story called "A Lady in Infra-Red," written when he was at Stanford. The background Steinbeck had collected in Panama provided scenery and atmosphere. The novel was more than a Caribbean pirate adventure. Steinbeck wanted to weave the nobility and magic of the Arthurian legend into his tale. King Arthur's knights had searched for the Holy Grail, the golden cup from which Jesus drank at the Last Supper, according to medieval legend. Steinbeck's pirate/knight is searching for an ideal, too. It would take years of working and reworking for Steinbeck to produce his manuscript, which was finally called *Cup of Gold.*

Cup of Gold was not Steinbeck's only writing project at the Brigham estate. For most of his life, he wrote short stories and articles while longer works were in progress. One of the first short stories he finished at the estate was "The Gifts of Iban," a fable set in an enchanted forest. The characters in this story are fairies, but it is not a children's story. Steinbeck submitted "The Gifts of Iban" to a new magazine called *The Smoker's Companion.*

Steinbeck welcomed the chance to write without interruptions or distractions, but he was sometimes lonely at the Brigham estate. When he could, he talked old friends from Stanford into coming for a visit. Twice a week, he went down to the local dock on Lake Tahoe to meet the mail boat. He was glad for the chance to talk to the boat captain as well as receive the mail.

In March 1927, the mail boat brought a letter from *The Smoker's Companion.* "The Gifts of Iban" had been accepted. It was Steinbeck's first national publication, but he thought so little of the magazine that he put a pen name, John Stern, on the story. It was John Steinbeck, however, who received the magazine's $15 payment.

In May 1927, the Brigham children and grandchildren returned to the Tahoe house for a visit. So

Steinbeck traveled to Stanford to see his friend Toby Street. Street was hoping to make a career as a playwright, but he was struggling with a work he called "The Green Lady." Finally Street decided the play was a lost cause. He gave the story to Steinbeck and suggested that Steinbeck turn it into a novel. Steinbeck accepted this gift, but "The Green Lady" would have to wait. First he wanted to finish writing a group of stories that would become his second book, *The Pastures of Heaven*. He still had *Cup of Gold* to finish, too.

Back at Lake Tahoe in January 1928, Steinbeck finally finished *Cup of Gold*. His Stanford friend Ted Miller was living in New York and agreed to take the manuscript around to publishing companies. It would be a whole year before Steinbeck would learn the manuscript's fate.

That March, a midnight snowstorm caused a tree to break through the roof of the main house at the Brigham estate. The crash woke Steinbeck, asleep in his cabin. Ignoring the danger he faced, he grabbed a flashlight and made his way to the main house. There he found the living room filled with snow, which continued to fall through a huge hole in the roof. Furniture and carpets were ruined. Steinbeck ignored them. In the cold and dark, he worked through the night, carrying armloads of the Brighams' precious books to safety in his own cabin.

The Brigham family did not blame Steinbeck for the accident to the roof. Obviously, there was no way he could have prevented it, and he did the best he could to prevent worse damage. Still, it was time for him to move on. Lloyd Shebley, who ran a government fish hatchery at nearby Lake Tallac, offered Steinbeck a job at the hatchery. Steinbeck settled in to live and work at the Tallac Hatchery in late May of 1928.

A few weeks later, Steinbeck was alone at the hatchery when two sisters who were vacationing in the area stopped by for a visit. Steinbeck led the sisters on a tour of the hatchery. He traded wisecracks along the way with the taller, more outgoing sister, Carol Henning. Twenty-two-year-old Carol had brown hair, blue eyes, and nice features. Her clothes and her personality showed her style, wit, and confidence, just as her humor did. Steinbeck liked her at once.

When Shebley returned to the hatchery, near evening, Steinbeck told him to get ready for their double date with the Henning sisters. Steinbeck's beat-up, thirteen-year-old Dodge roadster got three flat tires on the two-mile drive to the Henning sisters' hotel. The evening with Carol and Idell Henning began with laughter when Steinbeck and Shebley arrived late and grimy from repairing tires. The two men cleaned themselves up and took Carol and Idell out for dinner and dancing. After that, Carol and Steinbeck spent as much time together as possible. On July 4, the Henning sisters' ten-day vacation ended. Carol returned to her job in San Francisco.

Besides the work at the hatchery, John Steinbeck had three things on his mind the rest of that summer. He was still working on *The Pastures of Heaven*. He had started writing a novel version of Toby Street's "The Green Lady." And he was trying to figure out how to get Carol Henning back into his life. At summer's end, Steinbeck left the hatchery job. He moved to San Francisco so he could be near Carol.

Steinbeck got a job at a large bag factory in San Francisco. That solved the problem of getting close to Carol, and it provided money to live on. Unfortunately, the job left him with little time or energy to write. By December 1928, he had quit the factory and moved to his family's cottage in Pacific Grove, where he threw himself into writing. Carol was working in the advertising department of a San Francisco newspaper. She and Steinbeck could still see each other whenever she could make the 120-mile trip down to Pacific Grove.

That Christmas, Steinbeck's father made a present of his confidence in Steinbeck's writing. Steinbeck could continue to live rent-free at the Pacific Grove house and his father would give him an allowance of $25 a month as long as he needed it. It was not much money, even in 1928, but with vegetables in the garden and free fish in the ocean, Steinbeck could get by.

In January 1929, Steinbeck heard from Ted Miller in New York. Seven publishers had rejected *Cup of Gold*, but Miller had finally found one that said yes. The company agreed to pay Steinbeck $250 and to print 1,500 copies. It would be nearly a year before the book actually appeared in print, but Steinbeck had a publisher at last. It was Robert McBride and Company—the same firm that had turned Steinbeck away three years earlier.

Steinbeck was happy with this modest success, but it did not distract him from his work. He knew that a steady routine was the way to make progress. He rose each morning about seven, made coffee, and

John Steinbeck was attracted to Carol Henning's style, wit, and confidence.

headed for the dining table to begin his warm-up. Usually, the warm-up was a letter to one of his Stanford friends. Telephone calls were an expense he could not afford in 1929, but that was not the only reason he wrote letters. "I write instead of telephoning because I have never been able to communicate over the telephone," he once explained.[3] Steinbeck wrote thousands of letters during his lifetime, and nearly everyone who received letters from him saved them.

What usually did not get saved were early drafts of writing that Steinbeck did not want published. The fireplace devoured pages of his work on "The Green Lady." This was Steinbeck's main project in those days at the Pacific Grove house. He produced about one hundred pages and destroyed many more. Then he set that work aside to resume work on the stories for *The Pastures of Heaven*.

These stories are built around the Munroe family, who seem to introduce suffering into the lives of everyone they meet. In one story, a happy and talented young teacher is driven away from the town by her fear of Bert Munroe's hired hand.[4] Another story has an aging and lonely bachelor, haunted by the ghosts of his demanding parents, secretly in love with Mae Munroe. The ghosts return when his hopes of marrying Mae are dashed.[5] Through it all, the Munroes have no idea of the pain they bring into other people's lives.

In the fall of 1929, Steinbeck and Carol Henning decided they would move to southern California at the end of the year and get married there. Steinbeck's friends were happy with his choice. Carol was smart and independent with a sense of humor to match Steinbeck's. She had confidence in his future as a writer and did not object to his poverty, Steinbeck said.

A few weeks after Steinbeck and Carol announced their engagement, the stock market crashed. The Great Depression began with the October 1929 crash. Before this financial crisis was over, millions of Americans would be unemployed and poor. "The Depression was no financial shock to me," Steinbeck recalled years later. "I didn't have any money to lose."[6]

On January 14, 1930, John Steinbeck and Carol Henning were married by a judge in Glendale, near Los Angeles. They rented a run-down cottage in the neighboring town of Eagle Rock. The rent was cheap— $15 a month—but the place needed many repairs. Steinbeck's father raised his allowance from $25 to $50 a month after he married. This did not leave much money to spend on repairs to the cottage. Steinbeck bought parts and materials at junkyards, and he and Carol did most of the work themselves.

Neither Steinbeck nor Carol had regular jobs at first. When they were not sanding floors or replacing pipes, Carol was editing and typing Steinbeck's manuscripts and discussing business possibilities with some friends. Steinbeck had returned to working on "The Green Lady," which he was now calling "To an Unknown God."

Most of the story Toby Street had given him was gone from Steinbeck's manuscript now. Street's green lady had become a launching point for Steinbeck's own story about Joseph Wayne and his efforts to control nature. When Steinbeck finished the new version in

March, he sent it off to Robert McBride and Company. It was promptly rejected.

After two months, John and Carol had their rented house in good shape. The landlord stopped by to visit and agreed that they had done a fine job of improving the place. In fact, it was good enough now for his own newly married son to move in. The Steinbecks would have to leave.

Steinbeck and Carol moved to a more expensive place just north of Eagle Rock. Steinbeck bought an open 1923 Chevrolet with a leaky radiator. The trick was to keep it running without spending money on repairs. A handful of cornmeal added to the radiator was supposed to be a way to stop leaks. "The hot water cooked the meal to mush and it plugged the leak," Steinbeck explained.[7] Then one day the car overheated in Los Angeles. The radiator cap flew off and mush came gushing over the windshield. Carol was splattered but not injured.

Steinbeck would later turn this incident into stories for two magazines. In the first one, "A Model T Named It," the car became a Model T, the cornmeal became oatmeal, and the mush-splattered passenger became his mother.[8] In a later story, "Jalopies I Cursed and Loved," the car was an open Chevrolet again—"a black bathtub on wheels." Steinbeck described meeting his beautifully dressed mother at the train station. He began to drive her to his home. . . .

Suddenly there was an explosion—a wall of oatmeal rose into the air, cleared the windshield, splashed on my mother's hat and ran down her face. . . . We went through Los Angeles traffic exploding oatmeal in short bursts. I didn't dare stop for fear my mother would kill me in the street.[9]

Early in 1930, Carol Steinbeck abandoned her plans to start a business. She began to look for a regular job. Through the spring and summer Steinbeck worked on a new manuscript he called "Dissonant Symphony." It would eventually wind up in the fireplace. By August, the reality of the Depression had set in for both Steinbecks. Carol could not find a job. "To an Unknown God" could not find a publisher. John and Carol moved back up north to Pacific Grove, where they could at least live without paying rent.

4

Depression Days

The Steinbecks were poor but happy in Pacific Grove. They shared meals and cheap good times with a growing circle of friends and neighbors. One of these was a marine biologist named Ed Ricketts, who operated a small laboratory in Pacific Grove. He collected and preserved specimens from the tide pools of Monterey Bay and sold them to schools for their science classes. Sometimes Steinbeck helped with this work. Other times, he simply hung out at the lab with Ricketts, talking science and philosophy. Ricketts would become the model for characters in several Steinbeck works, including *In Dubious Battle, Cannery Row*, and *Sweet Thursday*.

Steinbeck also found story ideas in Ricketts's lab.

Steinbeck and marine biologist Ed Ricketts, above, became lifelong friends.

One of the early ones became "The Snake." Steinbeck included it in a collection called *The Long Valley*, published in 1938. In that story a well-dressed, slightly mysterious woman visits the lab and asks to buy a live snake. She does not want to take it with her. She just wants to come to the lab now and then to watch her snake eat a live rat. "When I wrote the story just as it happened, there were curious reactions," Steinbeck recalled. "One librarian wrote that it was . . . the worst story she had ever read. A number of orders came in for snakes."[1]

Steinbeck and Ricketts became lifelong friends. Their conversations helped Steinbeck refine some of his ideas about the role that luck plays in the lives of all creatures, including humans. Collecting specimens with Ricketts in the tide pools of Monterey Bay, Steinbeck might notice that a small shrimp had just become a meal for a larger creature. That was bad luck for the shrimp, but necessary for the overall survival of the tiny world of the tide pool. There was no blame to be assigned. It was just how the world is. Steinbeck called this "Is" thinking. Later Ricketts would teach him a longer name—"non-teleological thinking"—but the idea was the same. The goal was not to figure out what caused an event, or what that event might bring about in the future, but to focus on things as they are in a single slice of time. This way of seeing things would be important in many of Steinbeck's later works, including *Of Mice and Men*, *The Grapes of Wrath*, and *The Pearl*.

Another idea that Steinbeck sometimes explored with Ricketts was the difference between the way an

Ed Ricketts, right, shows a small ray to a visitor in his marine biology laboratory in Pacific Grove.

individual acts alone and as part of a group. He remembered reading about ancient armies whose soldiers would march close together with their shields held overhead. The shields created a sort of shell that protected all the soldiers from arrows or rocks hurled by an enemy. This formation was called a *phalanx*, from the Greek word for turtle. The massed shields gave the group of soldiers something like the hard shell of a turtle as long as every soldier kept in step.

Steinbeck saw a similar pattern in nature. A school of fish, for example, enjoyed greater safety as long as all the fish stayed together. Moving as a single mass made them appear to be one very large creature that could scare off possible attackers. A fish that wandered away from the school was more likely to be eaten. If many fish wandered off, the whole school would be in danger. Sometimes, the same thing was true of humans. This phalanx idea would show up in such Steinbeck works as *In Dubious Battle* and *The Grapes of Wrath*.

Life in Pacific Grove settled into a happy routine. Ed Ricketts hired Carol Steinbeck to help with the lab's bookkeeping and correspondence. Steinbeck wrote in the mornings and spent afternoons talking with Ricketts or other friends. Listening to his Pacific Grove neighbors, he gathered ideas and details that he would use later in his writing. At the local used-car lot, he learned how to detect sawdust in the crankcase—a trick salesmen used to make a car run quieter for a few miles.[2] The tricks he learned at the used-car lot would one day find their way into *The Grapes of Wrath*. In the book, Al explains to his brother

Tom Joad how he inspected the car their family bought for the trip to California:

> *I gave the whole thing a good goin'-over 'fore we bought her. Didn' listen to the fella talkin' what a hell of a bargain she was. Stuck my finger in the differential and they wasn't no sawdust. Opened the gear box an' they wasn't no sawdust. . . .*[3]

Carol came home from Ricketts's lab each day to edit and type the pages Steinbeck had written. This was her contribution to the success she was sure Steinbeck would achieve. Steinbeck's job was to tell the stories, not to worry about spelling and punctuation. He knew that his writing needed editing, but he was glad not to have to do it himself. Steinbeck had his own work to do, and the Depression often made it discouraging, as he recalled:

> *I went on writing—books, essays, short stories. Regularly they went out and just as regularly came back. Even if they had been good, they would have come back because publishers were hardest hit of all. When people are broke, the first things they give up are books.*[4]

In 1931 a little bit of good luck came Steinbeck's way. He had sent *The Pastures of Heaven* to a literary agent named Mavis McIntosh in New York. McIntosh and her partner Elizabeth Otis both liked the manuscript. They became Steinbeck's agents and soon had *The Pastures of Heaven* sold to a publishing firm. With encouragement from his new agents, Steinbeck rewrote "To an Unknown God" one more time. The new version, called *To a God Unknown*, was accepted by a publisher in 1932.

Steinbeck's parents were encouraging, too. His father urged local bookstores to stock John Steinbeck's works. His mother suggested that her reading club try one of his books. The club members turned her down flat. Steinbeck's subjects and characters were not wholesome enough for Salinas ladies.

In March 1933, Steinbeck's mother suffered a stroke that left her paralyzed. Steinbeck and Carol moved in with his father in Salinas. For weeks, Steinbeck sat silently by his mother's hospital bed. Not even the sound of his pen scratching on paper would disturb her, because he could not write. Then, slowly at first, he began to work on a short story about a young boy whose father surprises him with the gift of a pony. The story reached back to Steinbeck's own childhood. It captures the feelings of the boy, Jody Tiflin:

> *A red pony colt was looking at him. . . . Its tense ears were forward and a light of disobedience was in its eyes. Its coat was rough and thick as an Airedale's fur and its mane was long and tangled. Jody's throat collapsed on itself and cut his breath short.*[5]

McIntosh and Otis sold "The Red Pony" to the *North American Review*. That prestigious magazine paid Steinbeck $90. "The Red Pony" would become one of Steinbeck's best-known, best-loved, and most enduring stories. Eventually, Steinbeck would take his agents' advice and write more stories about the Tiflin family. "The Red Pony" (retitled "The Gift") would become the opening chapter in Steinbeck's short novel

"The Red Pony," one of Steinbeck's best-known and best-loved stories, is celebrated here in an exhibit at the National Steinbeck Center.

The Red Pony. It would also be included in dozens of short-story collections. Readers of the *North American Review* enjoyed "The Red Pony," and the editor asked Steinbeck for more stories.

The success of "The Red Pony" was about the only bright spot for Steinbeck in 1933. His mother had come home from the hospital, but she was not going to get well. Steinbeck's father became less and less able to care for himself. While a hired nurse looked after Olive Steinbeck, John escaped from the overwhelming sadness of the Salinas house by writing. The burden of caring for the elder Steinbecks and looking after the house fell more and more on Carol. At night, when the household and nursing chores were done, Carol edited and typed Steinbeck's manuscripts. Exhausted, Carol worried about money.

The Depression had everyone worrying about money. One in four Americans who wanted jobs could not find them. People who had jobs were afraid of losing them. To make matters worse, a severe drought in the Midwest was driving farm families off their land. Many were coming to California to look for work. Some had set up a camp near Salinas. With so many people wanting work, the ranch owners could lower the pay they offered. The migrant workers were too desperate to turn down any amount. Their hardship and fear were a constant reminder of the country's terrible financial problems. The Steinbecks were safe for the moment, but could they stay safe?

By the end of 1933, Steinbeck had three novels and several short stories published, but his writing had brought in less than $1,000. "Every time a publisher accepted one of my books, he went bankrupt," Steinbeck wrote.[6] In addition to more stories for *North American Review*, Steinbeck was working on a new novel, *Tortilla Flat*. He was racing now to become a successful writer before his parents died. It was a last chance to pay his father back for helping to support him. It was a last chance to thank his mother for trying to get her friends to read his books.

Olive Steinbeck died on February 19, 1934. Steinbeck and Carol moved with John's father back to the cottage in Pacific Grove. The smaller house was slightly less work for Carol, but John's father needed more and more of Carol's attention and care.

In March Steinbeck finished writing *Tortilla Flat* and sent it off to McIntosh and Otis. The book's ideas were lifted straight from Malory's *Morte d'Arthur*, but Steinbeck had changed the characters. Instead of medieval knights, they were a band of Mexican immigrants who lived near Monterey in an area known as Tortilla Flat. Like the language of medieval knights, their speech is full of "thees" and "thous." Like medieval knights, they care deeply about honor.

In Steinbeck's story, these *paisanos*, as the Mexican immigrants are called, live mostly by their wits. They work when they absolutely have to. More often they get food and wine by tricking their neighbors into giving it to them. When one of them, Danny, inherits two houses, he rents one house to the other *paisanos*. Danny and his tenants all know the rent will never be paid, for the *paisanos* have no money. They all know it is dishonorable not to pay the rent. They also know it is dishonorable for Danny to hound them for the rent. This problem of honor is solved when the *paisanos* accidentally burn down the rented house and move in with Danny in the only house he has left.[7]

Throughout *Tortilla Flat*, the *paisanos'* comic adventures echo the episodes, language, and themes of the Arthurian legend. These "knights" turn conventional ideas about honor upside down, but there is something noble about them. McIntosh and Otis did not understand this book, but they agreed to try to find a publisher for it.

Steinbeck began working on a new novel, *In Dubious Battle*. On the largest ranches in California, the pay for migrant field-workers kept going down. Some ranch owners even looked for ways to cheat the workers out of the little pay they did earn. They would claim a worker owed rent for having stayed a few nights on the ranch and deduct that amount from the worker's pay. The powerless workers had little choice but to accept whatever money they could get.

Now and then a few of the workers would try to organize the whole group on a ranch. They could refuse to harvest a crop unless the pay was higher. If all the workers stuck together in a strike, the ranch owner would have to raise the pay or watch his crop rot in the field. This was Steinbeck's idea of the phalanx in action.

The ranchers helped one another fight back whenever a strike was threatened. They told the newspapers that the strikes were organized by Communists. The Communist Party said that the people who do the work ought to get the benefits. It was wrong for the ranch owners to hire workers at the lowest possible wages, sell the crops at the highest possible price, and keep all the profit. The very idea of communism frightened most Americans, but the hard times of the Depression made some think that the Communists might be right. Why, they wondered, should the landowners keep getting richer while the people who actually did the work stayed poor?

What happens in *In Dubious Battle* is like what was actually happening on some California ranches in the 1930s. In the book, Mac, an organizer from the Communist Party, leads a group of migrant fruit pickers in a strike. What Mac really wants is to gain supporters for the Communist Party and its ideas, no matter who or what must be sacrificed. His friend Jim wants to improve the lot of the migrant workers. A strike is a dangerous way to try to do that, but Jim is willing to face the risks if necessary. Doc Burton, another important character in the book, is based partly on Ed Ricketts. He tries to see this situation as it is, without looking for its cause or deciding who is to blame.[8] Steinbeck was putting his ideas about the phalanx and "Is" thinking together in one dramatic book.

Two thousand miles away, in Chicago, a different sort of drama was taking place. A book publisher named Pascal ("Pat") Covici had stopped in at the Argus Bookshop to visit the owner, Ben Abramson. Abramson was raving about the work of a little-known writer, John Steinbeck. Covici agreed to have a look at Steinbeck's work. He left the store with a copy of *The Pastures of Heaven*. Abramson was right, Covici decided. He phoned McIntosh and Otis to ask

Steinbeck's novel In Dubious Battle *is about migrant fruit pickers who strike for better pay—much like these real-life cotton workers on strike in California in 1933.*

if they had anything else by Steinbeck that he could see. As a matter of fact, they did. Covici bought the rights to *Tortilla Flat*. The publishers of *To a God Unknown* and *The Pastures of Heaven* had gone out of business, so Covici arranged for his company, Covici-Friede, to reissue those books as well as publish *Tortilla Flat*.

At last, John Steinbeck had a publisher who believed in him. He hoped now that his father would live long enough to see him become a successful writer. It was not to be. John Ernst Steinbeck died on May 23, 1935. *Tortilla Flat* was published five days later. It was indeed the book that made Steinbeck a successful writer. It sold four thousand copies—more than Steinbeck's three earlier novels put together. Steinbeck wrote later that the book "was bought for motion pictures for $3,000. I had no conception of this kind of dough. It was like thinking in terms of light-years."[9]

Trampling Out the Vintage

People were talking about *Tortilla Flat* and John Steinbeck. Not everyone who was talking about *Tortilla Flat* liked it. Some Monterey residents felt that Steinbeck embarrassed their town by glorifying people they saw as lazy and even criminal. People who did like the book thought Steinbeck would be happy if they dropped by his house to tell him so. The interruptions distracted Steinbeck from what he really wanted and needed to do—finish writing *In Dubious Battle*.

The attention disturbed Carol, too. Once the new manuscript was done, in August 1935, Steinbeck and Carol drove to Mexico for a vacation. They both needed to get away from all the attention Steinbeck was getting. The Steinbecks liked Mexico and its people, and they stayed three months. They returned to Pacific Grove in late December. The attention they had tried to escape had not gone away.

In Dubious Battle came out in January 1936. Some critics complained that the book made the farmworkers and strike organizers look bad. Others complained that the book made the farm owners look greedy and mean. Steinbeck did not bother to answer the critics. The whole point of "Is" thinking was not to take sides. If the critics disagreed about whose side Steinbeck was on, he must have got it right.

Steinbeck began planning his next book—or trying to, between interruptions. What he had in mind was a combination novel and play, a book that could be acted out on a stage. *Of Mice and Men* was Steinbeck's first attempt to combine a novel and a play. It would be a story about working men, for working men. The title came from a line in "To a Mouse," a poem by the Scottish writer Robert Burns: "The best-laid schemes o' mice an' men gang aft agley." This means that sometimes bad things just happen, no matter how carefully you plan.

Carol thought of a way she and Steinbeck could regain their privacy, now that they had some money. They bought a piece of property a little farther north, in Los Gatos, just a few miles south of San Jose, where Carol had grown up. Carol began supervising the construction of a house she had designed.

By the time *Of Mice and Men* was finished, so was the Los Gatos house. Pat Covici liked the new manuscript, and the Steinbecks liked their new house. The house was not large, only eight hundred square feet, but it included a small workroom for Steinbeck. Carol decorated the rooms with bright colors and some of the clay sculptures she had brought back from Mexico. When the weather was just right— warm and dry—the new place reminded Carol and John of the happy times they had spent on their Mexican vacation.

In August 1936, Steinbeck was ready to begin a new project. George West, a friend from the *San Francisco News*, offered him one. West asked Steinbeck to visit migrant farmworkers like the ones he had described in *In Dubious Battle* and tell their story in a series of seven articles for the newspaper.

To research the newspaper series, Steinbeck needed to travel to the camps where the migrant workers lived. These were called "squatters' camps." They sprang up in fields and on roadsides throughout the farming regions of California. Families traveling in search of work would camp for a few nights wherever they could find space and water. Those who had tents slept in them. Others created lean-tos by stretching tattered blankets from their cars to create roofs they could sleep under. The poorest just lay down on the open ground. There were no bathrooms or showers, and illnesses spread quickly among the families in a squatters' camp.

Steinbeck did not want to call too much attention to himself when he visited the camps. He purchased an old bakery truck and filled it with clothes, bedding, and food, making a sort of camper that he called the "pie wagon."[1] His travels in the pie wagon introduced

Migrant workers set up "squatters' camps" in fields and along the roadsides. These camps had no bathrooms or showers, and diseases spread quickly.

Steinbeck to the troubles of the migrant workers and to one man who was helping at least some of them. That man was Tom Collins.

The federal government had sent Tom Collins to set up a "sanitary camp" near Marysville, California. If the Marysville camp succeeded, the government would build others. Tall and thin, intelligent and hardworking, Tom Collins kept detailed records about the families who came to the sanitary camp. The reports told how many people were in each family, where they came from, whether any of them were ill, and how many could work in the fields. They also told whether the family had any money, or even any food. Collins shared this information with Steinbeck.

At the Marysville camp, about two thousand migrant workers could stay in cabins and have access to clean water for drinking and bathing. The camp had flush toilets and a vegetable garden that helped to feed all the families. There were games and some schooling for the younger children who were not out working in the nearby fields and orchards. There were even Saturday night dances for everyone at the camp.

The men and older children staying in the Marysville camp walked or rode out at daybreak to harvest crops on nearby ranches. They worked hard until sundown and received only pennies for a day's work. The mothers of young children stayed behind at the camp while their husbands and older children worked in the fields. These women tended the camp's vegetable garden, cleaned camp facilities, repaired clothing, and prepared meals. Life was not easy for the families in the sanitary camp, but it was better than in the squatters' camps.

When the Marysville camp appeared to be successful, Tom Collins set up another camp, the Arvin Sanitary Camp, called "Weedpatch." It was located near Bakersfield, California, about 350 miles from Marysville. Collins took Steinbeck through both of these camps. Collins introduced Steinbeck to some of the families and showed him written reports about others.

Steinbeck's newspaper series appeared in October 1936. It was called "The Harvest Gypsies." It gave a brief history of California's reliance on migrant workers

Tom Collins, above, created "sanitary camps" to improve living conditions for migrant farmworkers and their families.

for harvesting. Over several decades, Steinbeck wrote, California had depended on waves of immigrants— from China, Japan, the Philippines, and Mexico—to do this work. The latest wave of workers were not immigrants. They came from America, from the Dust Bowl states of Oklahoma, Arkansas, Texas, and Kansas. Unlike the earlier groups, these workers brought their wives and children. They earned barely enough to feed their families. There was never enough to pay for medical care when poor diet or filthy living conditions made them sick. In one of the articles, Steinbeck traced the spiral of decline that such families suffered. In the space of a year, the "loss of dignity and spirit" brought newcomers to a "state of subhumanity," he wrote.[2]

"Dignity," Steinbeck explained, did not refer to a man's feelings about himself. Rather, he said, it was "a register of a man's responsibility to the community." Dignity was what the migrant experience had "kicked out of" the harvest gypsies.[3]

Steinbeck wrote that the families in the sanitary camps had begun to regain their sense of responsibility to the larger group—their dignity. He believed this was a sensible way to provide the temporary workers the big ranch owners needed without trampling on the workers. In the last article of the "Harvest Gypsies" series, he said so. Steinbeck mapped out his own plan for creating communities in which "a spirit of cooperation and self-help" is "encouraged and supported by the federal and state governments."[4]

Steinbeck wanted to do more to help the migrant families. In December 1936, he began to plan a book that would make the migrants' experience real to American readers. He would call it "The Oklahomans."

Planning for that new book was interrupted when Broadway producer George S. Kaufman wrote to Steinbeck in March 1937. Kaufman wanted to produce a stage version of *Of Mice and Men*, but he did not feel that a play could be lifted directly from the book, as Steinbeck had intended. He wanted Steinbeck to help him write a script for a Broadway play. The Steinbecks were on their way to visit Sweden, Denmark, and Russia. On their way back they spent a week at Kaufman's farm in Pennsylvania. Steinbeck and Kaufman worked on the play. In October, the Steinbecks bought a car and drove home to California.

On this last part of the journey, Steinbeck absorbed the look and feel of the highways in the middle part of America. The scene in the lower Midwest was unforgettable. On either side of Route 66, where farms had been, there was dry brown earth. The long drought in this part of the country had ruined the crops of farmers who were already poor because of the Depression. Then the winds came. They blew away the dry topsoil in dust storms, so there could be no crop the next year even if it did finally rain. When the bankrupted farmers could not repay their loans, the banks took the farms, and the families had to leave.

The Steinbecks sometimes found themselves driving alongside dilapidated cars and trucks piled high with household belongings. These were farm families from Arkansas and Oklahoma, on their way to California, to look for field work and a new start. "The Oklahomans" would tell their story.

The winter of 1937–1938 was rainy in northern California. Floods turned one squatters' camp near Visalia into a muddy swamp. People there were dying of smallpox and starvation. By February 1938, Steinbeck was angry. He abandoned "The Oklahomans" and began furiously writing a nasty satire he called "L'Affaire Lettuceberg." By mid-May, this seventy-thousand-word manuscript was done, but he wrote to Elizabeth Otis that he had destroyed it. "My father would have called it a smart-alec book," he wrote. "It was full of tricks to make people ridiculous."[5]

By writing down the Lettuceberg version of the migrants' story, Steinbeck had got the anger out of his head. Now he could write the massive and moving story of what he had seen on Route 66, in the California camps, and in the migrants' faces. Steinbeck started the new version on May 31, 1938.

That same day, he began keeping a journal of his progress. Each day, he recorded the time he began, which scene or chapter he was working on, and whether the day's writing was easy or difficult. The journal also tells who or what distracted him from the work. Several new houses had been built around Arroyo del Ajo since 1936. When the neighbors were not shouting, they were hammering. The washing machine was making noise. Carol had to have her tonsils taken out. One friend or another was coming to visit. There were negotiations to buy a new piece of property. Plans for a new house had to be made, and builders had to be hired. Almost every entry in

In rickety trucks piled high with their possessions, farm laborers traveled about in search of work. Steinbeck knew that he wanted to tell their story.

Steinbeck's journal ends with a sentence or two, such as, "I must get down to it now and prove to myself that I can still concentrate no matter how badly. Time to go now. Get to it and fight it through."[6]

This novel would tell the story of Tom Joad, the grown-up son of poor, honest Oklahoma farmers. Tom returns from prison just in time to find that his family is about to leave home in search of farmwork in California. They have seen printed flyers promising plenty of work and good wages in the faraway state. Persuading a former preacher named Jim Casy to come along, the family heads west in a battered old car that has been converted into a truck. Sickness, death, and car troubles along the way use up much of the Joads' money, but they meet other migrant families worse off than they are. In California they discover that the promises about work and wages were lies. Hunger and disease are everywhere in the squatters' camps. The situation is only a little better in the sanitary camp where the Joads stop for a while. Finally, a flood claims their truck—their one link to the next job up the road. Tom decides that organizing the workers is the only way to make a better life, not just for his family but for all the migrant families. That decision makes Tom a fugitive, a hunted man. His mother is left to lead the family, with little more than her own faith that they will survive. "We ain't gonna die out," she says. "People is goin' on—changin' a little, maybe, but goin' right on."[7]

Steinbeck had no title for the new book, but this story was almost fully formed in his head before he began to write. He set to work each day, usually around 11:00 A.M., knowing exactly which part of the story came next. In his journal, he warned himself not to rush. Slowly, Steinbeck filled two ledger pages a day with tiny handwriting. Each eighteen-by-twelve-inch page held about one thousand words. When Steinbeck had written about one third of the manuscript, Carol began editing and typing the copy that would be sent to McIntosh and Otis. One week later, Steinbeck wrote in his journal: "Carol got the title last night 'The Grapes of Wrath.' I think that is a wonderful title."[8]

Steinbeck finished drafting *The Grapes of Wrath* on October 26, 1938, exactly one hundred working days after he had begun. He and Carol moved into their still-unfinished new house, on the forty-seven-acre Biddle Ranch outside Los Gatos. In the new house, Carol finished typing the 751-page manuscript. Then she and Steinbeck made final corrections. On December 7, 1938, the manuscript was mailed to McIntosh and Otis.

Covici-Friede had gone out of business while Steinbeck was writing *The Grapes of Wrath*. Pat Covici was now an editor at Viking Press. *The Grapes of Wrath* was the first John Steinbeck title published by Viking. It came out on April 14, 1939, with a dedication to Carol, "who willed this book," and to Tom Collins, "who lived it."[9]

The Grapes of Wrath aroused controversy immediately. The controversy was not about the book as literature, but about whether it was true. California ranchers and farm organizations claimed the book was entirely made up, and full of lies. The migrant

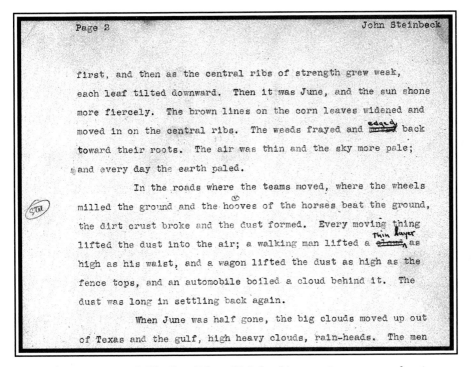

Page 2   John Steinbeck

first, and then as the central ribs of strength grew weak, each leaf tilted downward. Then it was June, and the sun shone more fiercely. The brown lines on the corn leaves widened and moved in on the central ribs. The weeds frayed and edged back toward their roots. The air was thin and the sky more pale; and every day the earth paled.

In the roads where the teams moved, where the wheels milled the ground and the hooves of the horses beat the ground, the dirt crust broke and the dust formed. Every moving thing lifted the dust into the air; a walking man lifted a thin layer as high as his waist, and a wagon lifted the dust as high as the fence tops, and an automobile boiled a cloud behind it. The dust was long in settling back again.

When June was half gone, the big clouds moved up out of Texas and the gulf, high heavy clouds, rain-heads. The men

The Grapes of Wrath, *John Steinbeck's moving saga about migrant workers, poured from his pen. Then Carol Steinbeck typed the 751-page manuscript. Page 2, above, shows some editing changes marked by John Steinbeck himself.*

workers' lives were nowhere near as bad as Steinbeck's story made them look, the growers said.[10]

Newspapers and magazines sent their own reporters to the camps to see for themselves. *Life* magazine printed photographs taken in the migrant camps. Eleanor Roosevelt, the wife of President Franklin D. Roosevelt, reported in her newspaper column about conditions in the camps she visited. They were every bit as bad as what Steinbeck described, the first lady wrote. Movie producer Darryl F. Zanuck bought the rights to film *The Grapes of Wrath*. Zanuck secretly sent private detectives to the camps to find out if they were as awful as Steinbeck's book made them seem. The camps were worse, the detectives reported.

The Grapes of Wrath was a huge success. Viking printed 480,000 copies in the first year. When the Pulitzer Prizes were announced in May 1940, *The Grapes of Wrath* was honored as 1939's best novel. It remains one of the biggest-selling books of all time.[11]

6

Explorations

$\mathbf{F}$or the rest of 1939, *The Grapes of Wrath* brought John Steinbeck more fame and attention than he thought possible. Even in the new house, remote as it was, the interruptions never stopped. The lack of privacy upset Carol as much as Steinbeck. They had to get away. He needed to clear his mind for the next project. Steinbeck's friend Ed Ricketts had published a book of his own in 1939, an important work on marine biology. Ricketts wanted to get away for a while, too.

Steinbeck and Ricketts hired a sardine-fishing boat, the *Western Flyer*. They planned to collect specimens of plants and animals in Mexico's Gulf of California. The *Western Flyer* left Monterey on Monday afternoon, March 11, 1940.[1] Carol was the only woman on board. Steinbeck hoped that including her in this work might solve the problems his fame seemed to cause in their marriage. Steinbeck and Carol had been a good team in their early years together, but now she appeared to feel left out and resentful.[2]

By the morning of March 17, Steinbeck, Carol, and Ricketts—plus three crewmen and the captain who owned the *Western Flyer*—had reached Cape San Lucas, at the southern tip of Baja California, a part of Mexico. For the next four weeks, the *Western Flyer* visited beaches along the shores of the Gulf of California. The boat's crew met villagers and ten-foot manta rays, tricky sea currents and rough weather.

On shore they sometimes heard gunfire and often heard stories, including one about a young diver who had found an enormous pearl. At first the diver and his neighbors celebrated his good fortune. As envy and greed took over, the pearl brought more and more bad luck to the diver. Finally the diver reclaimed his simple, honest life by throwing the pearl back into the ocean. This tale would become the basis for Steinbeck's short novel *The Pearl*.

Gradually, the *Western Flyer* worked its way up the western shore of the Gulf of California and then down the eastern shore. At each stop Steinbeck and the others collected crabs, worms, urchins, anemones, sponges, corals, and hundreds of other specimens. They watched how the tide-pool creatures moved about, what they ate, and how they protected themselves.

When they could not collect specimens, Steinbeck

and Ricketts were busy in the laboratory they had set up on board the *Western Flyer*. There they preserved the specimens they had collected. They tried different ways of killing and preserving the creatures to make the best specimens. They discovered that if they put certain kinds of worms into a container with a fish, seawater, and a little air, the worms would eat all the soft flesh and leave a perfect fish skeleton.[3]

Steinbeck promised McIntosh and Otis that he and Ricketts would write a book about their trip after they returned. The book's title would be one of the old names for the Gulf of California, *Sea of Cortez*. First, though, Steinbeck looked for a way to help people like those he had met in Mexico.

Some of the remote villages the *Western Flyer* visited had no doctors at all. The villagers knew nothing of modern methods to keep their drinking water pure and safe. Impure water caused illnesses that swept through an entire village, sickening and even killing the weakest residents. The people in such villages relied on a local *curandera*, or wise woman, to conduct rituals that would drive away the "bad airs" that had brought illness to their families. They did not trust modern medicine, even when it was offered to them.[4]

Steinbeck thought he could help these people by telling their story in a movie. Instead of setting to work with Ed Ricketts on *Sea of Cortez*, Steinbeck returned to Mexico to write and film *The Forgotten Village*. Ricketts was unhappy to have Steinbeck leave their project and go work on something else.

Ricketts was also unhappy because the new

Steinbeck poses with Captain Berry on the Western Flyer. *Cruising on the Gulf of California, Steinbeck, along with his wife and Ed Ricketts, studied crabs, worms, urchins, and hundreds of other sea creatures.*

project was the very opposite of "Is" thinking. Here was Steinbeck looking for causes and trying to change a situation. The Mexican villagers' poverty and misery were caused by their lack of education. Steinbeck hoped that making this film would bring education and modern medicine to Mexico's remote villages. That could change the future for the villagers. That kind of meddling with the world was exactly what "Is" thinking rejected.

The Forgotten Village was the first movie script Steinbeck wrote. Other people had made movies from his books, including *Of Mice and Men* and *The Grapes of Wrath*. Steinbeck had become friends with some of the filmmakers. They encouraged him to write movies. One of them—actor Burgess Meredith—was the off-screen narrator for *The Forgotten Village*. Except for Meredith, Steinbeck's first movie had no professional actors. The villagers who were in it spoke little or no English. That did not matter, for they had no lines to speak. Meredith's voice told the story while the people on the screen acted out the events he described.[5] When the filming was finished, Steinbeck returned to the *Sea of Cortez* project.

Sea of Cortez has two parts: a "log," or narrative portion, and a more technical marine science report. People assumed that Steinbeck had written the narrative and Ricketts had written the scientific part of the book. Both men said that was not true. They worked together on both parts, they said. Steinbeck was proud of the contribution *Sea of Cortez* made to science. Years later, Steinbeck told a British magazine writer, "At one time a very eminent zoologist said that the two of us together were the best zoologists in America."[6]

The trip had not solved the problems in Steinbeck's marriage. John and Carol Steinbeck separated in April 1941. By the time he finished writing *Sea of Cortez*, Steinbeck had removed every mention of Carol from the book. There was no doubt now that they would get a divorce. In September, Steinbeck moved to New York City. It would be easier for Carol to start a new life, he thought, if the two of them did not live in the same town.

Sea of Cortez was published on December 5, 1941. Two days later, Japanese planes bombed Pearl Harbor and other American military bases in Hawaii. The United States entered World War II the next day, and Steinbeck looked for a way to serve his country. He decided to use his writing ability in the service of the United States and its allies. The U.S. Army Air Corps accepted his offer, and he wrote *Bombs Away: The Story of a Bomber Team*, which was published in 1942.

Steinbeck's next book was *The Moon Is Down*, a novel about the heroics of ordinary citizens who resist a takeover of their unnamed country by an unnamed army. The invaded country resembled Norway, and the story had many parallels to the recent Nazi occupation of that country. In Steinbeck's story, the powerful invading army overwhelms the defenses of the small, peace-loving country and makes military resistance impossible. The country's only hope lies in individual acts of heroism, spying, and sabotage.

The Moon Is Down was propaganda—writing that

Steinbeck kept his promise to write a book about his boat trip on the Western Flyer. The Sea of Cortez, *both a sea log and a marine science report, was coauthored with Ed Ricketts.*

aims to shape readers' opinions. It did not seem to be in the same class with the literary novels Steinbeck had written before the war. It did what it was meant to do, however. *The Moon Is Down* was credited with helping morale during World War II, in Norway and other countries fighting the Nazis.

Meanwhile, Pat Covici was getting anxious. It had been four years since *The Grapes of Wrath* was published. Steinbeck's experiments with nonfiction, films, and propaganda were interesting, maybe even noble. Wasn't it time now to write another novel?

A Season of Loss

While he waited for his divorce from Carol to become final, John Steinbeck had been seeing an actress and singer named Gwyn Conger. Gwyn enjoyed Steinbeck's celebrity and was happy to socialize with his show-biz friends. Steinbeck admired and respected the work of his stage and film friends, but he still preferred to stay out of the limelight. Their different ideas about Steinbeck's fame did not stand in the way of a wedding. On March 29, 1943, Steinbeck and Gwyn were married in New Orleans. Gwyn began furnishing and decorating their New York townhouse. Steinbeck prepared to go overseas as a war correspondent for the *New York Herald Tribune*.[1]

Steinbeck and Gwyn had been married less than ten weeks when he left for Europe. Gwyn was soon feeling lonely and neglected. She wanted her husband to come home.

Steinbeck returned from Europe in October 1943. He was depressed about the death and destruction he had seen. By December he had begun planning a new novel, *Cannery Row*. Set in Monterey, this would be a funny, lighthearted story featuring a scientist known as Doc, who kept a laboratory in Monterey. It would lift readers' spirits. It would lift Steinbeck's own spirits.

The planning of *Cannery Row* had barely begun when Steinbeck decided a trip to Mexico would really cheer him up. He wanted to follow up on the story about the diver who found an enormous pearl. Steinbeck and Gwyn spent two months in sunny Mexico in early 1944. Steinbeck continued to think about *Cannery Row* while he absorbed the details of village life for *The Pearl*. As those two stories took shape in his mind, another idea was forming: He wanted to move back to California.

Back in New York in March, the Steinbecks learned Gwyn was pregnant. They decided to stay in New York until after their first child was born. Steinbeck finished writing a screenplay, *Lifeboat*, for the famous director of suspense films, Alfred Hitchcock.

Lifeboat is about a group of passengers from a cruise ship that has been torpedoed by a Nazi submarine. The passengers must depend on one another—and trust one another—to survive in their lifeboat until they can be rescued. Luckily, one of the people they have pulled on board has the sailing skills to steer their boat toward rescue. Then they discover he is the captain from the Nazi submarine that sank their ship—and they begin to worry about the destination of their lifeboat.[2]

Thom Steinbeck was born August 2, 1944. In letters to friends, Steinbeck claimed not to be overly impressed with his son or with his new status as a father. He wrote to Dook Sheffield, "Neither of us are gaga but we're very glad to have him and we'll have some more."[3] The letter also outlines Steinbeck's happy plans to return to California. Steinbeck and his new family moved into their new Monterey home in October 1944.

In California, Steinbeck set to work on another movie, *A Medal for Benny*. This movie is forgotten today, but the screenplay was nominated for an Academy Award in 1946. Benny—who is never seen in the movie—is a bit of a bum. The citizens of his California hometown have run him out of town. Benny joined the army and has been killed. Now that Benny is a war hero, the townspeople decide that they loved and thought well of him. They are eager to accept a medal for him in a grand ceremony.[4]

Steinbeck liked people like Benny. They refuse to live up to the middle-class standards others try to set for them, but they harm no one. He distrusted the respectable townsfolk who made it their business to decide how other people ought to behave. In novels like *In Dubious Battle* and, later, *East of Eden*, he tried to show that such busybodies are hypocrites. In other works, including *Tortilla Flat* and *A Medal for Benny*, he poked fun at them.

In 1943, Steinbeck began planning a new novel, a funny, lighthearted story set in Monterey on Cannery Row, pictured here.

Cannery Row is full of characters like Benny. Mack and his friends take jobs now and then in the local cannery, but they are not career-minded. Like the *paisanos* of *Tortilla Flat*, they have simple tastes and little need to own the trappings of a middle-class life. They have the friendship of Doc, a marine biologist modeled on Ed Ricketts, and their lives are filled with comic misadventures. After one character, Lee Chong, becomes the owner of a warehouse near his grocery store, Mack and his friends offer to move into the place and keep an eye on it. Lee Chong suggests they pay rent of five dollars a week, but he knows he will never get the money. Lee Chong is not unhappy about this. In fact, Steinbeck writes:

> *Everyone was happy about it . . . you cannot steal from your benefactor. The saving to Lee Chong in cans of beans and tomatoes and milk and watermelons more than paid the rent.*[5]

When *Cannery Row* was published in January 1945, some Monterey residents saw it as another attempt by Steinbeck to embarrass the town. Steinbeck's money and stature as a writer should have made him one of the town's most respected citizens. Instead, the town's most respected citizens were often the ones who were most upset by what he wrote. The ordinary working people Steinbeck liked so much now kept their distance, too. They could not be themselves around the famous writer. Steinbeck could not be himself around them. Steinbeck still enjoyed Ed Ricketts's friendship, but some of his other friends had become jealous of his success.

Steinbeck hoped all that would change if he went away again. With Gwyn and Thom, he went to Mexico in April to work on the filming of *The Pearl*. By the end of 1945, he had begun working on his next novel, *The Wayward Bus*, and planning another film, about the life of the Mexican revolutionary Emiliano Zapata. Gwyn was expecting their second child, and the Steinbecks had purchased a new home in New York City.

They moved into the new townhouse in April 1946. Like it or not, Steinbeck was a New Yorker now. Steinbeck fit in there with a circle of friends more like the person he had become—a well-known and esteemed writer of books, plays, and movies. Gwyn, too, preferred New York and the friends they had made there.

Social activities were put aside because of Gwyn's pregnancy. She felt ill and unhappy most of the time. John Steinbeck IV was born on June 12, 1946, but Gwyn's illness and unhappiness did not end. Gwyn and Steinbeck both loved their sons, but Gwyn felt trapped as a housewife and mother. What she really wanted was a career in show business. Instead, she remained at home with her two young sons while Steinbeck returned to Mexico to finish work on the movie version of *The Pearl*.

After Steinbeck returned from Mexico, he treated Gwyn to a vacation in Europe. The trip did not go as Steinbeck had planned. He was the center of attention. *The Moon Is Down* had inspired people all over Europe during World War II. In Denmark, Sweden, and France, people flocked to meet the admired

John and Gwyn Steinbeck chat with Jack Wagner, right, who helped with the filming of Steinbeck's story The Pearl *in Mexico in 1945.*

American author. In Norway, Steinbeck was awarded the King Haakon Liberty Cross. Only Norwegian resistance fighters had received the medal up to that time. For an American civilian to get the medal was a great honor. Gwyn did not attend the ceremony with Steinbeck. After four weeks in Europe, Gwyn was ready to go home. She missed Thom and John IV, she said.

In June 1947, Steinbeck and Gwyn returned to Europe for another monthlong vacation. While Gwyn went home to New York alone, Steinbeck hooked up with the famous war photographer Robert Capa. The two men had arranged to tour Russia, the Ukraine, and Georgia—three of the republics in what was then the Soviet Union. They would spend four months together, gathering material for *A Russian Journal*. Capa's photographs would illustrate Steinbeck's words about the large nation that was a mystery to most Americans.

Steinbeck stayed in New York less than three months after his return from Russia. In February 1948, he headed for California to research his next novel. It would be about the Salinas Valley. He looked through old copies of the Salinas newspaper. He interviewed people who had lived in the Salinas Valley a long time. He visited old friends and family members. He spent time with Ed Ricketts and began planning another marine science book with him. Also, he escaped from Gwyn and the increasing tension in their marriage. Steinbeck returned to New York in March, but he and Gwyn spent little time together.

Steinbeck planned to go back to California in July. Perhaps Gwyn and the boys would come, too. Then Steinbeck and Ricketts would sail up to the Queen Charlotte Islands off the western coast of Canada. This expedition would produce their next book about the marine life of the Pacific Ocean.

On the night of May 7, 1948, Ed Ricketts was driving across a "blind" railroad crossing in Monterey. He could not see the train that was speeding along the curve of the tracks. His car was so noisy he could not hear the train either. The curve of the tracks made it impossible for the engineer to see Ricketts's car. There was no way to avoid the crash. Steinbeck left New

York as soon as he got the news, but by the time he arrived on May 11, Ricketts was dead.

Steinbeck did not speak at Ed Ricketts's funeral. Shocked with grief, he sat outside the chapel with other friends, silently watching the ocean waves throughout the memorial service.[6] Many years later Steinbeck told an interviewer that he had been "destroyed" by Ricketts's death. Ricketts, Steinbeck said, "was my partner for eighteen years—he was part of my brain."[7]

Ed Ricketts's death was not the only shock for Steinbeck that May. When he returned to New York after the funeral, Gwyn told him she wanted a divorce. Steinbeck moved into a hotel. He made repeated trips to Mexico. In September he moved back to the house in Pacific Grove. He was researching his movie script on Emiliano Zapata, he said. He was working on his big novel about the Salinas Valley, he said. In letters and late-night conversations, though, he hinted at the thing he could not say—he was not writing, could not write, at all.

The Fair Elaine

John Steinbeck finally returned to the script for *Viva Zapata!* in the spring of 1949. He wrote several sketches and stories for the novel he was now calling "The Salinas Valley." He began to think about another play/novelette, an experimental, mystical work called *Burning Bright.* He was looking forward to having his sons spend the summer with him. He was socializing again, especially on frequent trips to Los Angeles, where he became friends with the actress Ann Sothern.

Steinbeck invited Ann Sothern to come to Pacific Grove for Memorial Day weekend in 1949. She brought along a friend, Elaine Anderson Scott. Elaine Scott was attractive, smart, and funny. She had had a successful career as a Broadway stage manager when she lived in New York. Steinbeck liked her immediately.

Elaine Scott lived near Los Angeles now, and Steinbeck still lived in Pacific Grove. Scott had a teen-age daughter, Waverly, to look after. Steinbeck had four-year-old Thom and three-year-old John IV, now known as "Catbird," with him for the summer. Picnics and beach outings with all three children gave Steinbeck and Scott their best chance to be together and get to know each other.

Steinbeck set aside his work projects for the summer to focus on being with his sons. He took them out on boats and introduced them to fishing. He cooked for the boys, too, as he reported in a letter to Elaine Scott:

> *I am going to make my world-shaking macaroni for dinner and the kids are wild with joy because it means that there will be tomato sauce all over the kitchen and all over me. My dinners are not only food. They are decorations also.*[1]

After the boys returned to their mother's home in New York, Steinbeck got back to work on *Viva Zapata!* He had written hundreds of pages for this project, but they were not in the shape of a screenplay yet. Producer Darryl F. Zanuck and director Elia Kazan were eager to start filming. It was time to stop writing background and produce a script. In November 1949, Zanuck's assistant, Jules Buck, came to Pacific Grove to help.

By now Steinbeck knew Emiliano Zapata's story by heart. Zapata was a young Mexican peasant with no money and no education. All he had was the courage to speak up for his neighbors when powerful men stole their land. One dictator after another double-crossed Zapata, but his courage inspired others. Believing in Zapata, the peasants found their own courage and fought on after his death.[2]

Something clicked when Jules Buck arrived. Steinbeck quickly began dictating big chunks of the screenplay while Buck typed furiously. Now and then Steinbeck paused to draw sketches of how a scene should look. The draft script was complete in less than two weeks. This was a breakthrough. For two years Steinbeck had struggled to produce a new long work. He had written sketches and background material for several works but no actual manuscript for anything. Here at last was a whole film script.

The script was far from perfect. Steinbeck and Elia Kazan would work on and off for more than a year on revisions. *Viva Zapata!* would become Steinbeck's best film ever, and his last. After the movie was released in 1952, it would bring Academy Award nominations to Steinbeck, for best screenplay, and to two of the movie's stars, Marlon Brando and Anthony Quinn. Quinn, who plays Zapata's brother, won the award for best supporting actor.

By Christmas of 1949, Steinbeck and Scott had moved to New York. Scott and her daughter lived in an apartment in the same building where Steinbeck had rented a small penthouse. Steinbeck resumed work on *Burning Bright*. Like *Viva Zapata!* this play and novel had been jammed up in his brain during those two awful years. Just like the Zapata script, the draft of *Burning Bright* came together quickly now.

Through Elaine Scott, Steinbeck met the Broadway producers Richard Rodgers and Oscar Hammerstein II. Scott had been the stage manager for one of their most famous productions, *Oklahoma!* Rodgers and Hammerstein agreed to produce *Burning Bright*. After the play opened in October, Steinbeck wrote frankly to a friend, "The critics murdered us."[3]

The failure of *Burning Bright* disappointed Steinbeck, but he did not spend much time worrying about it. He and Elaine Scott were married on December 18, 1950. They bought a house on East Seventy-second Street in New York City and began setting up a home. Scott's daughter, Waverly, would live with them most of the year, and Steinbeck's sons, Thom and Catbird, could spend weekends and school holidays with them.

Steinbeck was already back at work on "The Salinas Valley." This novel would achieve greatness, Steinbeck believed. "This is the book I have always wanted and have worked and prayed to be able to write," he told Pat Covici.[4]

Steinbeck wrote the novel on the right-hand pages of a blank book Covici had given him. On the left-hand pages he kept a journal about the process of writing the book, just as he had done while working on *The Grapes of Wrath*. The journal was written as a series of letters to Covici, even though Covici would not read any of them until the novel was finished. The journal begins with Steinbeck explaining to Covici that the novel will be written "to my sons."[5] They were far too young at the time to read it, but they would read it someday. It would tell them the story of their ancestors' early days in the Salinas Valley, said Steinbeck, but it would also tell

> *the story of good and evil, of strength and weakness, of love and hate, of beauty and ugliness. I shall try to demonstrate to them how these doubles are inseparable—how neither can exist without the other and how out of their groupings creativeness is born.*[6]

Steinbeck began the novel believing that he would tell the stories of two early Salinas Valley families—the Hamiltons and the Trasks. Some Hamilton characters were named for and modeled on Steinbeck's own relatives. The Trasks were a completely fictional family. Their story was patterned after the biblical story of Adam and Eve and their sons Cain and Abel.

As Steinbeck worked on the novel from February to November 1951, the Trask story seemed to take over. When he revised the draft in the winter of 1951–1952, only a few Hamilton characters remained. The main story is about Cal Trask's attempts to win the love and approval of his father, Adam, who seems to favor Cal's brother, Aron.[7]

Like the Trask story line, the title Steinbeck finally chose—*East of Eden*—came from the Bible. In Genesis 4:16, after Cain killed his brother, he lived in exile "in the land of Nod, on the east of Eden," out of God's presence. *East of Eden* is more than a retelling of Bible stories, however. It is also a saga about the settlement and development of the Salinas Valley. Minor plot twists and turns reveal some of the community leaders to be selfish and greedy. Once again, Steinbeck had produced a novel that some of the respectable citizens of Monterey County would resent.

All through the writing and revision of *East of Eden*, Elaine Steinbeck helped her husband by managing their home, looking after the children, and keeping things quiet so that Steinbeck could write without interruptions or distractions. The whole family spent the summer of 1951 on Nantucket Island. There Elaine entertained houseguests as well as the children and tutored Thom and Catbird.

The book revisions were finished in the spring of 1952, and Steinbeck and his wife took a six-month European vacation. He planned to write travel sketches along the way for *Collier's* magazine. Elaine Steinbeck agreed to take photographs for the magazine. This was the first of many such trips the Steinbecks would take in the years to come. Besides taking pictures, Elaine managed the trips as she managed their home life. She relieved her husband of details like buying tickets and making hotel reservations.

John and Elaine Steinbeck traveled, usually together, through all the years of their marriage. Elaine told an editor that John "traveled more than he worked. Yet he was *always* writing *something*."[8] Writing travel sketches and essays was a change of pace for him. The articles he produced were not high literary art, he knew, but they kept him writing almost every day. That was a routine he did not want to give up. Besides, the articles usually brought in enough money to pay for the trips.

Visitors to the National Steinbeck Center can sit behind the wheel of this early automobile, used in the movie version of Steinbeck's best-selling East of Eden.

Steinbeck wrote that in places where neither of them spoke the local language, he and Elaine used

> *tourist sign language. . . . If you are explaining some-*
> *thing in English to a man who understands only*
> *Italian, you speak very loudly and slowly. . . . At the*
> *same time, you put your forefinger and thumb togeth-*
> *er and make a gentle, downward, pulling motion, as*
> *though you were milking a mouse.*[9]

The Steinbecks were back in New York by September. He was writing more travel sketches for *Collier's* and other magazines. One of these described his growing affection for New York, the city that had once "beaten the pants off" him.[10] Near the end of the article, he wrote:

> *New York is an ugly city, a dirty city. Its climate is a*
> *scandal . . . its traffic is madness, its competition is*
> *murderous. But there is one thing about it—once you*
> *have lived in New York and it has become your*
> *home, no place else is good enough.*[11]

Steinbeck was ready now to think of New York as home, but his writing often looked back to his younger days and to California. *East of Eden* was published in September and was soon number one on the best-seller list. He was trying to develop a musical play based on the Monterey characters from *Cannery Row*. Even his travel sketches provided opportunities to recall some incident from his youth. He wove this description of his mother's parents into his sketch of Ireland:

> *My grandfather . . . was really a great man, a man*
> *of sweet speech and sweet courtesy. . . . His little*

John and Elaine Steinbeck visit a Paris shooting gallery with Steinbeck's sons, Thom and Catbird, in 1954.

*bog-trotting wife . . . put out milk for the leprechauns
. . . and when a groundling neighbor suggested the
cats drank it, she gave that neighbor a look that
burned off his nose.*[12]

Steinbeck spent 1953 working on more magazine articles and trying to write the musical. The idea was to use the *Cannery Row* characters—Doc, Lee Chong, Mack, and his friends—but to write a love story between Doc and a new female character. Steinbeck wrestled with the story for months, but he finally found he could not write the play. He wrote the story as a novel instead. It was published in 1954 as *Sweet Thursday*. Rodgers and Hammerstein produced a musical version, called *Pipe Dream*, in 1955. Parts of *Sweet Thursday* also found their way into a 1982 movie titled *Cannery Row*.

In September 1953, the Steinbecks rented a house in Sag Harbor, an old whaling town near the eastern tip of New York's Long Island. Steinbeck loved being near the ocean again. He could fish, swim, and sail here. On weekends he could introduce his sons to the outdoors and the sea, the life he remembered from when he was a boy.

John and Elaine Steinbeck spent nearly all of 1954 in Europe. They rented a house in Paris. Thom, Catbird, and Waverly came for the summer. Paris began to feel like home as Steinbeck got to know his neighbors and took his sons to fish in the Seine River, which runs through the city. He wrote articles for the French paper *Le Figaro* and several American magazines. He also worked on some short stories. He tried to think of these short pieces as easier to write than novels or plays, but he finally admitted that writing them well took as much energy as the longer works.[13]

As Steinbeck began to think about his next book, he wanted to write something about his own time, not set in the past as all his other books had been. While in Paris, he also began to think about a story set in his homeland, the United States. The ideas he had that summer and fall would eventually turn into three books. The first of these was a fantasy/satire on modern French politics, *The Short Reign of Pippin IV*, published in 1957. The other two would take Steinbeck and his readers back to America—*The Winter of Our Discontent* and *Travels with Charley*.

When Knighthood Was in Flower

The Steinbecks returned to New York in time for Christmas. They spent the early months of 1955 looking for a country house they could buy in Sag Harbor. The house they chose was just a summer cottage when the Steinbecks bought it. It was not in the best shape, but it sat on a perfect piece of land. Steinbeck described it as

> a beautiful little point of land on the inland waters, a place called Bluff Point. . . . My point, just under two acres, is shaded by great oak trees of four varieties and there are many bushes and pines to edge it on the water side.[1]

Bluff Point was far enough from New York City to

provide privacy. It had a boat dock and space for a garden. There were seagulls and the smell of ocean salt in the air.

Steinbeck set to work winterizing the cottage so he and Elaine could stay there even during colder weather. Home improvement became a regular part of life at the Sag Harbor house. Steinbeck liked doing his own carpentry, and he could also hire help when he needed it. As the improvements progressed, the Steinbecks would spend more and more of each year in Sag Harbor.

Now Steinbeck's life was as calm and steady as it had ever been. After New Year's in the Caribbean each year, the Steinbecks would divide their time between New York City and Sag Harbor. The stays in Sag Harbor got longer as Steinbeck thickened the walls and added a furnace to the house there.

Steinbeck became "Editor at Large" for the weekly *Saturday Review*, and he began contributing several short articles a year to that magazine. He told his agent he was trying to write a large experimental novel, but other projects kept pushing it out of the way. One of these was *The Short Reign of Pippin IV*. Another was a short story, "How Mr. Hogan Robbed a Bank," which was published in *The Atlantic Monthly* in March 1956. That story would turn into the seed for his novel *The Winter of Our Discontent*.

At the end of 1956, Steinbeck decided to translate *Morte d'Arthur* into modern English. He wrote an introduction to the work, explaining that he wanted to set the stories down *in plain present-day speech for my own young sons, and for other sons not so young . . . who are impatient with the difficulties of Malory's spelling and use of archaic words. If I can do this and keep the wonder and the magic, I shall be pleased and gratified.*[2]

Steinbeck began doing research on different versions of the Arthurian legend at New York libraries and museums. In 1957, the Steinbecks went to Italy so he could do research there. In 1958, they made a research trip to England. During this 1958 trip, Steinbeck discovered that he needed more time there. Before he even got back to New York, he was making plans to spend most of 1959 in Somerset, England, where the adventures of King Arthur and his knights took place.

One thing the house in Sag Harbor did not have was a quiet place for Steinbeck to write. He tried writing in the garage. He tried writing in the family car. He tried to set up a portable office on his boat. Nothing worked. Finally, in 1958, he designed and built a little six-sided office, which he named "Joyous Garde." The name came from *Morte d'Arthur*. Joyous Garde is the castle where Sir Lancelot takes Queen Guinevere.

Standing alone away from the house, Joyous Garde had everything Steinbeck needed to work. Its six walls were lined with shelves above and below the windows and a space for the drafting table he used as a desk. The place was so small that every book, pencil, and stapler was within Steinbeck's reach while he sat in his desk chair. It was too small for a second chair, so any visitor who did drop in would not stay long.[3]

Steinbeck and Elaine stayed in Somerset from February to October of 1959. The stone-walled Discove Cottage, where they lived, was hundreds of years old. All around them were the streams, hills, forts, and castles King Arthur himself had known. Steinbeck was eager to see exactly how these places looked and to imagine how they might have looked to King Arthur. From Somerset, the Steinbecks explored other parts of England and Wales where Arthur and his knights were believed to have traveled. Steinbeck worked steadily on the manuscript, but it was not coming together the way he had hoped.

Soon after the Steinbecks returned to New York, Steinbeck suffered a mild stroke. He spent two weeks in the hospital at the end of 1959 before he could continue his recovery at home. Even after he was well again, the struggle to tell the Arthurian legend was too much. He put the manuscript aside, hoping he might return to it one day.

By spring of 1960, Steinbeck was fully recovered. He began writing *The Winter of Our Discontent* on Easter Sunday. He finished the novel July 9. Once again, Steinbeck was writing about the shortcomings of the respectable middle class, but this story was different. Respectable, middle-class Ethan Allen Hawley is a store clerk in a small northeastern town. *The Winter of Our Discontent* is told from Hawley's point of view, so his values are not ridiculed or attacked. This time, Steinbeck seems to feel sorry for the man who does not have the courage to do the right thing.[4]

Steinbeck still wanted to get out into the country and see how Americans lived in the small towns and cities of the Midwest and the South. He knew how to do this. He had done it years before in his pie wagon. This time he could afford a better vehicle.

Steinbeck's 1960 version of the pie wagon was a pickup truck, with a comfortable camper installed in the back. Some of Steinbeck's friends thought the trip was a silly idea. They compared him to the crazy hero of *Don Quixote*, a sixteenth-century novel by the Spanish writer Miguel Cervantes. Steinbeck named his camper truck Rocinante, after Don Quixote's horse.[5] Steinbeck could sleep, eat, and read in the camper. He could write letters and make notes in his journal when he stopped for the night.

Steinbeck worried that the people he would meet would not be themselves if they knew he was a writer, so he adopted a sort of disguise for the trip. He brought along shotguns and fishing rods because "if a man is going hunting or fishing his purpose is understood and even applauded."[6] He dressed like an outdoorsman, too, topping off his boots and khaki pants with

a hunting coat with corduroy cuffs and collar and a game pocket in the rear big enough to smuggle an Indian princess into a Y.M.C.A. My cap was a blue serge British naval cap with a short visor and on its peak the royal lion and unicorn. . . .[7]

With his big blue-gray poodle, Charley, for company, Steinbeck drove away from the Sag Harbor house on September 23, 1960. He drove up through New England first. Steinbeck chatted with strangers wherever he went. Some of his talks inspired memories of his younger days. These are woven into the book that he wrote about this trip, *Travels with Charley in Search of America.*

Steinbeck had not laid out any particular plan or schedule for the trip, but one place he definitely wanted to visit was Sauk Centre, Minnesota. It had been the home of the novelist Sinclair Lewis, who wrote several books based on life in his own hometown. Lewis was the first American writer to win the Nobel Prize for Literature. That prestigious international award was set up by the Swedish industrialist Alfred Nobel. It is the most celebrated prize any writer can win. The citizens of Sauk Centre had not been proud of Lewis. They felt he had embarrassed them and their town in his novels.

Sinclair Lewis had been dead almost ten years when Steinbeck visited Sauk Centre. The town had put up a sign, "Birthplace of Sinclair Lewis." Sauk Centre now welcomed tourists who came for no reason except that Lewis had lived there.[8]

Steinbeck's tour of America included a short stop in Pacific Grove, to visit his sister Beth. A reporter from *The Monterey Peninsula Herald* came to interview Steinbeck. Did Steinbeck think he might move back to Pacific Grove someday? No, Steinbeck answered. "I used to walk down the street and know everybody I met. Now I'm a stranger."[9] On his way out of town, Steinbeck drove to the top of Fremont's Peak and stood looking down the Salinas Valley, remembering how much he had loved this place. Then he got back into Rocinante and drove away.[10] By the time he reached Virginia, Steinbeck had lost his taste for this road adventure. He wanted to go home—to New York.[11]

The long road trip left Steinbeck with mixed feelings about America and Americans. He had seen too much greed and self-centeredness, but he had also met people who seemed wise, willing, and able to do the right thing. Steinbeck had mixed feelings about himself, too. He was glad that he had stayed healthy and strong throughout the trip. Still, he was fifty-nine years old now. How many years did he have left?

While his health and energy allowed, Steinbeck wanted to take his sons on a long trip and show them at least some of the world. The family left in September 1961 for a round-the-world tour. Because the boys would be missing school, they took along a tutor named Terrence McNally. McNally would one day become a famous playwright himself. Together, Steinbeck and McNally planned the boys' studies to match the trip. They began in England, with Thom and Catbird reading *Morte d'Arthur* while they visited places Steinbeck had explored in 1959.

The plan changed drastically in November, when Steinbeck suffered an apparent heart attack in Italy. The family moved into a villa on the island of Capri. Steinbeck and his wife stayed at the villa while he recovered. McNally took Thom, seventeen, and Catbird, fifteen, on short trips to other European countries.

By May, Steinbeck was well enough to travel again, and the whole family went to Greece. There Steinbeck proudly allowed his sons to lead him on an informative tour of ancient ruins. Catbird explained

In 1960, John Steinbeck and his big poodle, Charley, traveled across America in this pickup truck/camper, which has now been restored and polished to a shine for display at the National Steinbeck Center.

the Greek history and mythology he had learned from McNally. It was evidence that Steinbeck's learn-by-traveling plan worked. He would have liked to continue around the world. The whole family was concerned about Steinbeck's health by now, and the boys needed to get back to New York for summer school. After they toured Greece, the Steinbecks headed home.

10

The Prize,
The Politics

On the morning of October 25, 1962, John Steinbeck turned on the television set in Sag Harbor and heard a news announcer declare, "John Steinbeck has been awarded the Nobel Prize for Literature." The news surprised Steinbeck. He had not known that he was being considered that year for the most important literary prize in the world.[1] Elaine forgot all about the breakfast she was in the middle of cooking. She took the pan of bacon off the stove and stuck it in the refrigerator. Then she and Steinbeck danced happily around their kitchen.

Their joy did not last long. By the next morning, some critics were declaring that Steinbeck did not deserve the award. Steinbeck had written nothing important since *The Grapes of Wrath*, they said. Even that novel, they sniffed, was not really worthy of the Nobel Prize. Steinbeck had a few defenders, but editorials in important newspapers and magazines dismissed him. A *New York Times* editorial called Steinbeck a writer who

> produced his major work more than two decades ago. . . . We think it interesting that the laurel was not awarded to a writer . . . whose significance, influence and sheer body of work had already made a more profound impression on the literature of our age.[2]

These attacks hurt. Worse, Steinbeck began to worry about whether he would ever write anything important after the award. Five American writers had won the Nobel Prize—Sinclair Lewis in 1930, Eugene O'Neill in 1936, Pearl Buck in 1938, William Faulkner in 1949, and Ernest Hemingway in 1954. All of them had written their best work before the award. None, Steinbeck believed, had written anything important after the award. Was there a curse attached to the Nobel Prize? Would it strike him, too?

Steinbeck hoped his acceptance speech could quiet his critics. He worked hard on it all through November. It was a short speech. Steinbeck avoided talking about himself in a personal way. Instead, he talked about "the writer," as if he were talking about writers in general. What he knew and said about "the writer" was drawn from his own experience. The speech was about him, but he tried to make it seem as if it were about all writers.[3] The writer's job, he said, is to expose human faults and failures and dredge up

> *our dark and dangerous dreams for the purpose of improvement. Furthermore, the writer is delegated to declare and to celebrate man's proven capacity for greatness of heart and spirit—for gallantry in defeat, for courage, compassion and love.*[4]

After the awards ceremony, Steinbeck gave a radio interview for the Swedish Broadcasting Corporation. "How do you look upon yourself as an author?" he was asked. In the studio with only a few people present, Steinbeck answered: "I don't think I have ever considered myself an author. I've considered myself a writer because that's what I do. I don't know what an author does."[5] This simple, unrehearsed statement got to the heart of Steinbeck's message: A writer writes. A writer may choose, as Steinbeck did, to use different forms—novels, short stories, plays, movies, and journalism. A writer may choose factual stories or fictional ones, but writing them down is the creative work.

John and Elaine Steinbeck continued to travel. He continued to look for new ideas. They made trips to Europe, the Soviet Union, and Israel. He sold articles about these trips to newspapers and magazines. A series of moving essays about America in the 1960s became a book, *America and Americans*, illustrated with pictures by some of the nation's best photographers. The book draws on Steinbeck's experiences during the *Travels with Charley* trip. It includes new versions of some of the same stories. *America and*

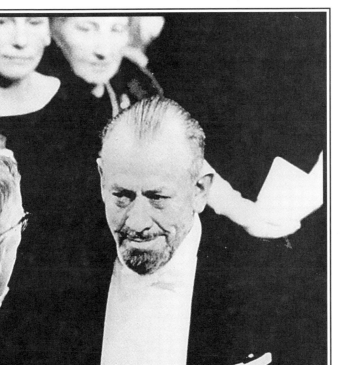

Steinbeck accepts the Nobel Prize for Literature at the awards ceremony in Sweden in 1962. In his speech, he said a writer's job was to expose human faults and dredge up "dark and dangerous dreams for the purpose of improvement."

Americans came out in 1966. It was the last Steinbeck book published during his lifetime.

Steinbeck recognized America's weaknesses in *America and Americans*, as he had in *Travels with Charley*. He was convinced that Americans would find the strength and courage to solve the nation's problems. By sticking together, Americans could lick any problem, from racial prejudice to poverty.

One big problem in the 1960s was the threat to world peace caused by hostility between the United States and Communist countries. The United States had sent troops to Southeast Asia to stop North Vietnamese Communists from taking over South Vietnam. More and more Americans believed the war was wrong and that the U.S. troops should leave South Vietnam. As public opposition to the Vietnam War grew, Steinbeck continued to support President Lyndon Johnson and the national policy that kept the war going.

In 1966, President Johnson suggested that Steinbeck go to Vietnam and see the war effort for himself. Steinbeck's son John IV—Catbird—now twenty, was serving with the Armed Forces Radio and Television Service in Vietnam. He was Steinbeck's guide. Elaine Steinbeck went along, too, but she stayed in a hotel in South Vietnam's capital, Saigon.[6] Steinbeck went to the war zone. He talked with officers and ordinary soldiers in the field. He sent reports back to the Long Island newspaper *Newsday*.

Five weeks in Vietnam left Steinbeck feeling that the war was a mistake. In his *Newsday* columns, however, he still said that Americans needed to stick together behind their government. Public opposition to the war was harmful. It was dividing the country in ways that might not heal even when the war was over.

John and Elaine Steinbeck flew to Bangkok, Thailand, in January 1967. Bangkok was close enough that John could return quickly if something "big" happened in Vietnam.[7] They traveled to other parts of Thailand and then to other troubled Southeast Asian countries.

By April, the Steinbecks were in Hong Kong, a peaceful oasis in a part of the world where danger and conflict were everywhere. They were relieved to be away from the constant threat of shelling and gunfire. They were enjoying the everyday routines of Hong Kong when Steinbeck stopped one day to help a man move a hand truck full of beer cases up some stairs. That was how, in calm and peaceful Hong Kong, Steinbeck injured his back.

Steinbeck thought he only had a slipped disk, and he was feeling better by the time he and Elaine returned to Sag Harbor the next month. Then his back went out again, and X rays revealed that the disk had ruptured. The doctors did not want to operate because of Steinbeck's age and his history of heart trouble. They put him in traction for two weeks. For the rest of the summer, he was in pain and in bed much of the time. Then his back went out again. This time the doctors decided to operate.

The operation was a success, but Steinbeck's health continued to worsen. A slight stroke and two heart attacks in late 1967 and early 1968 left him weaker and weaker. Steinbeck hated being in the hospital. He wanted to go home to Sag Harbor. Elaine had oxygen tanks brought into their house, and John's nurses taught her what to do in case of an emergency. With Elaine for his nurse, John was able to spend the summer and early fall of 1968 in the house he loved so well, but his writing days were over. In November, the Steinbecks returned to their home in New York City.

John Steinbeck suffered a heart attack and died on December 20, 1968. After a funeral service in New York, Elaine Steinbeck flew with her husband's ashes to California. She and Thom joined Steinbeck's sisters for another small service at Point Lobos, overlooking the Pacific Ocean. Then his ashes were buried in the Hamilton family plot at Garden of Memories Cemetery in Salinas.

Steinbeck's work continues to be published. Almost all of his books remain in print. Since Steinbeck's death, some of his unpublished manuscripts, diaries, and letters have been edited by others so they could be published.

The first of these was *Journal of a Novel: The East of Eden Letters*. Steinbeck believed his reports on the novel's progress revealed something useful about the process of writing. He had edited most of that work himself before his death, and the book came out in 1969.

Elaine Steinbeck asked editor and family friend Robert Wallsten to help her put together a collection of John Steinbeck's letters. The work of gathering, organizing, and editing thousands of saved letters took more than two years.[8] *Steinbeck: A Life in Letters* was published in 1975. The title has a double meaning that Steinbeck probably would have liked. In one sense, the title means "a life story revealed in the letters Steinbeck wrote." Another meaning of the phrase "a life in letters" is "a career in literature." In that sense, the title pays tribute to the quality of John Steinbeck's work.

Steinbeck's version of the Arthurian legends remained unfinished when he died. Steinbeck had loved this story since his childhood. It seemed wrong to leave the work unpublished. In 1974, Elaine Steinbeck turned the manuscript over to editor Chase Horton. *The Acts of King Arthur and His Noble Knights* was finally published in 1976.

Robert Wallsten and Chase Horton were just two of the scholars who developed a serious interest in Steinbeck's work. A Steinbeck Society was formed, and a journal about his work, *The Steinbeck Quarterly*, was started at Ball State University in Indiana. A Center for Steinbeck Studies was established at San Jose State University in California.

Even in Monterey County, John Steinbeck's reputation improved. Monterey's Ocean View Avenue was renamed Cannery Row. Salinas renamed its main library after Steinbeck and began holding an annual Steinbeck Festival. In 1993, Monterey officials purchased the lab where Steinbeck had spent so much time with Ed Ricketts. The old buildings that once stood next to the lab on Cannery Row have been torn down to allow expansion of the Monterey Aquarium. The huge modern aquarium now snuggles right up to the tiny weather-beaten lab.

The National Steinbeck Center at the north end of

The National Steinbeck Center in Salinas, California, pays tribute to America's author, John Steinbeck.

Main Street in Salinas houses Steinbeck memorabilia, including literary works. It has a theater, bookshop, and galleries with changing exhibits about the writer and the California he knew and loved. All of Monterey County celebrated the center's grand opening in June 1998. Local residents, it seemed, were eager to welcome John Steinbeck home.

Chronology

A list of Steinbeck's published works
appears on pages 115–117.

1902 — John Ernst Steinbeck III is born February 27 in Salinas, California.

1919 — Graduates from Salinas High School.

1919 — Attends Stanford University, taking classes in English literature, creative writing, and marine science.

1925 — Drops out of Stanford; works as a laborer and a reporter in New York.

1926 — Returns to California; continues to write, supporting himself with a variety of jobs.

1929 — First novel, *Cup of Gold*, is published.

1930 — Marries Carol Henning; meets marine biologist Edward F. Ricketts, who becomes a lifelong friend.

1931 — Begins selling his literary work through the McIntosh & Otis literary agency, New York.

1934 — Mother, Olive Hamilton Steinbeck, dies; short story "The Murder" wins O. Henry prize.

1935 — Father, John Ernst Steinbeck, dies; *Tortilla Flat*, his first major success, published; *Tortilla Flat* wins the Commonwealth Club of California Gold Medal.

1936 — Moves to Los Gatos; series of newspaper articles about migrant workers is published in *The San Francisco News*. *In Dubious Battle* wins a Gold Medal from the Commonwealth Club of California.

1937—*Of Mice and Men* is published as a novel in February; the stage play wins the New York Drama Critics' Circle Award; *The Red Pony* is published in three parts.

1939—*The Grapes of Wrath* is published; Steinbeck is elected to National Institute of Arts and Letters.

1940—*The Grapes of Wrath* wins a Pulitzer Prize; travels to the Gulf of California with Ed Ricketts.

1941—*Sea of Cortez: A Leisurely Journey of Travel and Research* is published, coauthored with Ed Ricketts; separates from Carol and moves to New York.

1943—Divorced from Carol Henning; marries Gwyn Conger; becomes war correspondent for the *New York Herald Tribune*.

1944—Son Thom is born; moves back to California.

1945—*Cannery Row* is published; *The Red Pony* is published with all four parts; returns to New York.

1946—Son John IV ("Catbird") is born; Steinbeck is awarded the King Haakon Liberty Cross (Norway) for *The Moon Is Down*.

1947—Travels through Russia with photographer Robert Capa, reporting for the *New York Herald Tribune*.

1948—Ed Ricketts dies; Steinbeck is divorced from Gwyn Conger and returns to California.

1950—Marries Elaine Scott in December; they live in New York.

1952—Correspondent abroad for *Collier's* magazine; film *Viva Zapata!* is released.

1954—Lives abroad for nine months; correspondent for *Le Figaro* and other publications.

1955—Buys summer cottage in Sag Harbor.

1957—Correspondent in Europe for Louisville *Courier-Journal* and syndicate; attends P.E.N. Congress in Tokyo.

1959—Lives most of the year in Somerset, England, studying *Morte d'Arthur.*

1960—Travels through the United States in a camper, with French poodle Charley.

1961—Begins ten-month trip abroad with his family.

1962—Receives the Nobel Prize for Literature.

1964—Receives the Presidential Medal of Freedom.

1966—Begins five-month trip through Southeast Asia as correspondent for *Newsday.*

1968—Dies in New York City on December 20.

1969—*Journal of a Novel: The East of Eden Letters*, his diary of the progress of *East of Eden*, is published.

1975—*Steinbeck: A Life in Letters* is published, edited by Elaine Steinbeck and Robert Wallsten.

1976—*The Acts of King Arthur and His Noble Knights*, Steinbeck's version of the *Morte d'Arthur*, is published.

1989—*Working Days: The Journal of a Novel [Grapes of Wrath]* is published.

Works by John Steinbeck

Fiction

Cup of Gold, 1929
The Pastures of Heaven, 1932
To a God Unknown, 1933
Tortilla Flat, 1935
In Dubious Battle, 1936
Of Mice and Men, 1937
The Red Pony, 1937
The Long Valley, 1938
The Grapes of Wrath, 1939
The Forgotten Village, 1941
The Moon Is Down, 1942
Cannery Row, 1945
The Wayward Bus, 1947
The Pearl, 1947
Burning Bright, 1950
East of Eden, 1952
Sweet Thursday, 1954
The Short Reign of Pippin IV: A Fabrication, 1957
The Winter of Our Discontent, 1961
The Acts of King Arthur and His Noble Knights, edited
    by Chase Horton, 1976

Nonfiction, a Selected List

*Sea of Cortez: A Leisurely Journal of Travel and
    Research*, with Edward F. Ricketts, 1941
Bombs Away: The Story of a Bomber Team, 1942

A Russian Journal (photographs by Robert Capa), 1948

"Critics, Critics, Burning Bright," *Saturday Review*, November 11, 1950, pp. 20–21

The Log from the Sea of Cortez, with "About Ed Ricketts," 1951

"Autobiography: Making of a New Yorker," *New York Times Magazine*, February 1, 1953, pp. 26–27, 66–67

"Jalopies I Cursed and Loved," *Holiday*, July 1954, pp. 45, 89–90

"Always Something to Do in Salinas," Holiday, June 1955, pp. 58–59, 152–153, 156

Once There Was a War (collected World War II correspondence), 1958

"A Primer on the Thirties," *Esquire*, June 1960 (reprinted October 1973, pp. 127, 129–131, 364, 366)

Travels with Charley in Search of America, 1962

America and Americans, 1966

Journal of a Novel: The East of Eden Letters, 1969

Steinbeck: A Life in Letters, edited by Elaine Steinbeck and Robert Wallsten, 1975

The Harvest Gypsies (1936 newspaper series), 1988

Working Days, The Journal of a Novel [The Grapes of Wrath], edited by Robert DeMott, 1989

Films and Plays

Of Mice and Men: A Play in Three Acts, 1937

Of Mice and Men (film based on the play), 1939

The Grapes of Wrath (film based on the novel), 1940

The Forgotten Village, screenplay by John Steinbeck, 1941

Tortilla Flat (film based on the novel), 1942
The Moon Is Down: A Play in Two Parts, 1942
The Moon Is Down (film from the play), 1942
Lifeboat, screenplay by John Steinbeck, 1944
A Medal for Benny, screenplay by John Steinbeck, 1945
John Steinbeck's The Pearl, screenplay by John Steinbeck, 1948
The Red Pony, screenplay by John Steinbeck, 1949
Burning Bright (play), 1950
Viva Zapata! screenplay by John Steinbeck, 1952
East of Eden (film based on the novel), 1954
Pipe Dream (Rodgers and Hammerstein musical based on *Sweet Thursday*), 1956
The Wayward Bus (film based on the novel), 1957
Flight (film based on the story), 1961
The Red Pony (film based on the stories), 1976
East of Eden (film based on the novel), 1980
Of Mice and Men (film based on the play), 1981
Cannery Row (film based on the novel), 1982
The Grapes of Wrath (play based on the novel), 1990
Of Mice and Men (film based on the play), 1992
Burning Bright (opera based on the play), 1993

Chapter 1. The Best-Laid Schemes o' Mice an' Men

1. Jackson J. Benson, *The True Adventures of John Steinbeck, Writer* (New York: Viking Press, 1984), pp. 325–326.

2. John Steinbeck, letter to Louis Paul, in *Steinbeck: A Life in Letters*, Elaine Steinbeck and Robert Wallsten, eds. (New York: Viking Press, 1975), p. 124.

3. John Steinbeck, letter to Elizabeth Otis, in *Steinbeck: A Life in Letters*, p. 124.

4. Benson, p. 330.

5. Nelson Valjean, *John Steinbeck, The Errant Knight: An Intimate Biography of His California Years* (San Francisco: Chronicle Books, 1975), p. 158.

Chapter 2. California Boy

1. John Steinbeck, letter to Mrs. Waverly Anderson, in *Steinbeck: A Life in Letters*, Elaine Steinbeck and Robert Wallsten, eds. (New York: Viking Press, 1975), p. 581.

2. Lewis Gannett, "John Steinbeck: Novelist at Work," *Atlantic*, December 1945, p. 55.

3. John Steinbeck, "Always Something to Do in Salinas," *Holiday*, June 1955, p. 58.

4. John Steinbeck, "Jalopies I Cursed and Loved," *Holiday*, July 1954, p. 45.

5. Jackson J. Benson, *The True Adventures of John Steinbeck, Writer* (New York: Viking Press, 1984), p. 21.

6. Steinbeck, "Always Something to Do in Salinas," p. 59.

7. Joseph Henry Jackson, "John Steinbeck: A Portrait," *Saturday Review*, September 25, 1937, p. 11.

8. Thomas Fensch, ed., *Conversations with John Steinbeck* (Jackson: University Press of Mississippi, 1988), p. xvii.

9. Nelson Valjean, *John Steinbeck, The Errant Knight: An Intimate Biography of His California Years* (San Francisco: Chronicle Books, 1975), p. 95.

10. John Steinbeck, letter to Edith Mirrielees, in R. S. Hughes, *John Steinbeck: A Study of the Short Fiction* (Boston: Twayne Publishers, 1989), p. 137.

Chapter 3. Years of Struggle

1. John Steinbeck, "Autobiography: Making of a New Yorker," *The New York Times Magazine*, February 1, 1953, p. 26.

2. Ibid., p. 27.

3. John Steinbeck, "Graduates: These Are Your Lives!" *Esquire*, September 1969, p. 69.

4. John Steinbeck, *The Pastures of Heaven* (New York: Covici-Friede, 1932), pp. 160–189; included as "Molly Morgan," in *The Portable Steinbeck.*

5. John Steinbeck, "Pat Humbert's," *The Pastures of Heaven*, pp. 216–245; included as "Pat Humbert's," in *The Portable Steinbeck.*

6. John Steinbeck, "A Primer on the Thirties," *Esquire*, October 1973 (reprinted from June 1960), p. 129.

7. John Steinbeck, "Jalopies I Cursed and Loved," *Holiday*, July 1954, p. 45.

8. Nelson Valjean, *John Steinbeck, The Errant Knight: An Intimate Biography of His California Years* (San Francisco: Chronicle Books, 1975), p. 131–132.

9. Steinbeck, "Jalopies I Cursed and Loved," p. 45.

Chapter 4. Depression Days

1. John Steinbeck, "About Ed Ricketts," in *The Log from the Sea of Cortez* (New York: Penguin Books, 1995), pp. 238–239.

2. John Steinbeck, "Jalopies I Cursed and Loved," *Holiday*, July 1954, p. 89.

3. John Steinbeck, *The Grapes of Wrath* (New York: Penguin Books, 1976), p. 130.

4. John Steinbeck, "A Primer on the Thirties," *Esquire*, October 1973 (reprinted from June 1960), p. 129.

5. John Steinbeck, *The Red Pony* (New York: Penguin, 1992), p. 9.

6. Steinbeck "A Primer on the Thirties," p. 364.

7. John Steinbeck, *Tortilla Flat* (New York: Penguin, 1986), pp. 55–56.

8. John Steinbeck, *In Dubious Battle* (New York: Covici-Friede, 1936).

9. Steinbeck, "A Primer on the Thirties," p. 364.

Chapter 5. Trampling Out the Vintage

1. Jackson J. Benson, *The True Adventures of John Steinbeck, Writer* (New York: Viking Press, 1984), p. 332.

2. John Steinbeck, *The Harvest Gypsies* (Berkeley: Heyday Books, 1988), p. 31.

3. Ibid., p. 39.

4. Ibid., p. 59.

5. John Steinbeck, letter to Elizabeth Otis, in *Steinbeck and His Critics*, E. W. Tedlock, Jr., and C. V. Wicker, eds. (Albuquerque: University of New Mexico Press, 1957), p. 33.

6. John Steinbeck, *Working Days: The Journals of The Grapes of Wrath*, Robert DeMott, ed. (New York: Penguin, 1989), p. 80.

7. John Steinbeck, *The Grapes of Wrath* (New York: Penguin Books, 1976), p. 542.

8. Steinbeck, *Working Days*, p. 65.

9. Steinbeck, *The Grapes of Wrath*, frontispiece.

10. Susan Shillinglaw, "California Answers *The Grapes of Wrath*" in *John Steinbeck: The Years of Greatness, 1936–1939*, Tetsumaro Hayashi, ed. (Tuscaloosa: University of Alabama Press, 1993), pp. 145–164.

11. National Steinbeck Center Web site <http://www.steinbeck.org/> (March 4, 1999).

Chapter 6. Explorations

1. John Steinbeck, *The Log from the Sea of Cortez* (New York: Penguin Books, 1995), p. 24.

2. Jay Parini, *John Steinbeck: A Biography* (New York: Henry Holt and Company, 1995), p. 232.

3. Steinbeck, p. 175.

4. John Steinbeck, screenwriter, *The Forgotten Village*, dir. Herbert Kline, Pan American Films, 1941. (Festival Films videocassette, 1983).

5. Herbert Kline, "The Forgotten Village: An Account of Film Making in Mexico," *Theatre Arts*, May 1941, pp. 336–343.

6. "Healthy Anger," *Books and Bookmen* (England), October 1958, reprinted in *Conversations with John Steinbeck*, Thomas Fensch, ed. (Jackson: University Press of Mississippi, 1988), p. 68.

Chapter 7. A Season of Loss

1. Jackson J. Benson, *The True Adventures of John Steinbeck, Writer* (New York: Viking Press, 1984), p. 516.

2. John Steinbeck, screenwriter, *Lifeboat*, dir. Alfred Hitchcock, Twentieth Century-Fox, 1944.

3. John Steinbeck, letter to Carlton A. Sheffield, in *Steinbeck: A Life in Letters*, Elaine Steinbeck and Robert Wallsten, eds. (New York: Viking Press, 1975), pp. 272–273.

4. All Movie Guide Web site <http://allmovie.com> (May 18, 1999).

5. John Steinbeck, *Cannery Row* (New York: Viking Press, 1945), pp. 9–10.

6. Benson, p. 615.

7. "Healthy Anger," *Books and Bookmen* (England), October 1958, reprinted in *Conversations with John Steinbeck*, Thomas Fensch, ed. (Jackson: University Press of Mississippi, 1988), p. 68.

Chapter 8. The Fair Elaine

1. John Steinbeck, letter to Elaine Scott, in *Steinbeck: A Life in Letters*, Elaine Steinbeck and Robert Wallsten, eds. (New York: Viking Press, 1975), p. 372.

2. Elia Kazan (director), *Viva Zapata!*, 1951 (Key Video, 1990).

3. Jackson J. Benson, *The True Adventures of John Steinbeck, Writer* (New York: Viking Press, 1984), p. 663.

4. John Steinbeck, *Journal of a Novel: The East of Eden Letters* (New York: Viking Press, 1969), p. 5.

5. Ibid., p. 4.

6. Ibid.

7. John Steinbeck, *East of Eden* (New York: Viking Press, 1952).

8. Pascal Covici, Jr., "Chronology," *The Portable Steinbeck* (New York: Penguin Books, 1976), p. xli.

9. John Steinbeck, "Duel Without Pistols, *Collier's,* August 23, 1952, p. 13.

10. John Steinbeck, "Autobiography: Making of a New Yorker," *The New York Times Magazine*, February 1, 1953, p. 27.

11. Ibid., p. 66.

12. John Steinbeck, "I Go Back to Ireland," *Collier's,* January 31, 1953, p. 49.

13. Benson, p. 766.

Chapter 9. When Knighthood Was in Flower

1. John Steinbeck, "My War with the Ospreys," *Holiday*, March 1957, p. 72.

2. John Steinbeck, *The Acts of King Arthur and His Noble Knights*, Chase Horton, ed. (New York: Noonday Press/Farrar Straus and Giroux, 1993), p. xiii.

3. Jackson J. Benson, *The True Adventures of John Steinbeck, Writer* (New York: Viking Press, 1984), pp. 789–791.

4. John Steinbeck, *The Winter of Our Discontent* (New York: Viking Press, 1961).

5. National Steinbeck Center Web site <http://www.steinbeck.org/center> (May 18, 1999).

6. John Steinbeck, *Travels with Charley in Search of America* (New York: Viking Press, 1962), p. 7.

7. Ibid., pp. 37–38.

8. Ibid., p. 120.

9. Mike Thomas, "John Steinbeck Back—But Not to Stay," *The Monterey Peninsula Herald*, November 4, 1960, reprinted in *Conversations with John Steinbeck*, Thomas Fensch, ed. (Jackson: University Press of Mississippi, 1988), p. 71.

10. Steinbeck, *Travels with Charley*, pp. 178–184.

11. Ibid., pp. 243–244.

Chapter 10. The Prize, The Politics

1. Jackson J. Benson, *The True Adventures of John Steinbeck, Writer* (New York: Viking Press, 1984), p. 914.

2. "Literature Award," editorial, *The New York Times*, October 26, 1962.

3. John Steinbeck, "Nobel Prize Acceptance Speech," *The Portable Steinbeck*, Pascal Covici, Jr. (New York: Penguin Books, 1976), pp. 690–692.

4. Ibid., p. 691.

5. Benson, epigraph, p. vii.

6. "The Press: Columnists: The Eye of the Veteran," *Time*, December 30, 1966, p. 41.

7. "Press: Steinbeck Up Front," *Newsweek*, January 30, 1967, p. 71.

8. Elaine Steinbeck and Robert Wallsten, eds., *Steinbeck: A Life in Letters* (New York: Viking Press, 1975), p. x.

Benson, Jackson. *The True Adventures of John Steinbeck, Writer.* New York: Viking Press, 1984.

Fensch, Thomas, ed. *Conversations with John Steinbeck.* Jackson: University Press of Mississippi, 1988.

Gannett, Lewis. "John Steinbeck: Novelist at Work," *Atlantic,* December 1945, pp. 55–60.

Reef, Catherine. *John Steinbeck.* New York: Clarion Books, 1996.

Stanley, Jerry. *Children of the Dust Bowl: The True Story of the School at Weedpatch Camp.* New York: Crown Publishers, 1992.

The Steinbeck Center Foundation. *Steinbeck Country: A Guide to Exploring John Steinbeck's Monterey County.* Salinas, Calif.: The Steinbeck Center Foundation, undated.

Steinbeck, Elaine, and Robert Wallsten, eds. *Steinbeck: A Life in Letters.* New York: Viking Press, 1975.

Valjean, Nelson. *John Steinbeck, The Errant Knight: An Intimate Biography of His California Years.* San Francisco: Chronicle Books, 1975.

Internet Addresses

Center for Steinbeck Studies at San Jose (California) State University home page

<http://www.sjsu.edu/depts/steinbec/srchome.html>

John Steinbeck page

<http://ocean.st.usm.edu/~wsimkins/steinb.html>

National Steinbeck Center home page provides links to a brief biography, a list of Steinbeck works (some with plot synopses), and information about the center and the Steinbeck Festival.
<http://www.steinbeck.org/index3.html>

"Rocinante" has details about the camper (now at the National Steinbeck Center in Salinas, California) Steinbeck used for his 1960 tour of the United States, recorded in *Travels with Charley in Search of America.*
<http://www.steinbeck.org/center/rocinante.html>

"Steinbeck Homes and Locations," Center for Steinbeck Studies photo tour of Steinbeck's California homes
<http://www.sjsu.edu/depts/steinbec/homhnts.html>

"Steinbeck: The California Novels," by Ed Stephan, has links to many related sites.
<http://www.ac.wwu.edu/~stephan/Steinbeck/>

Index